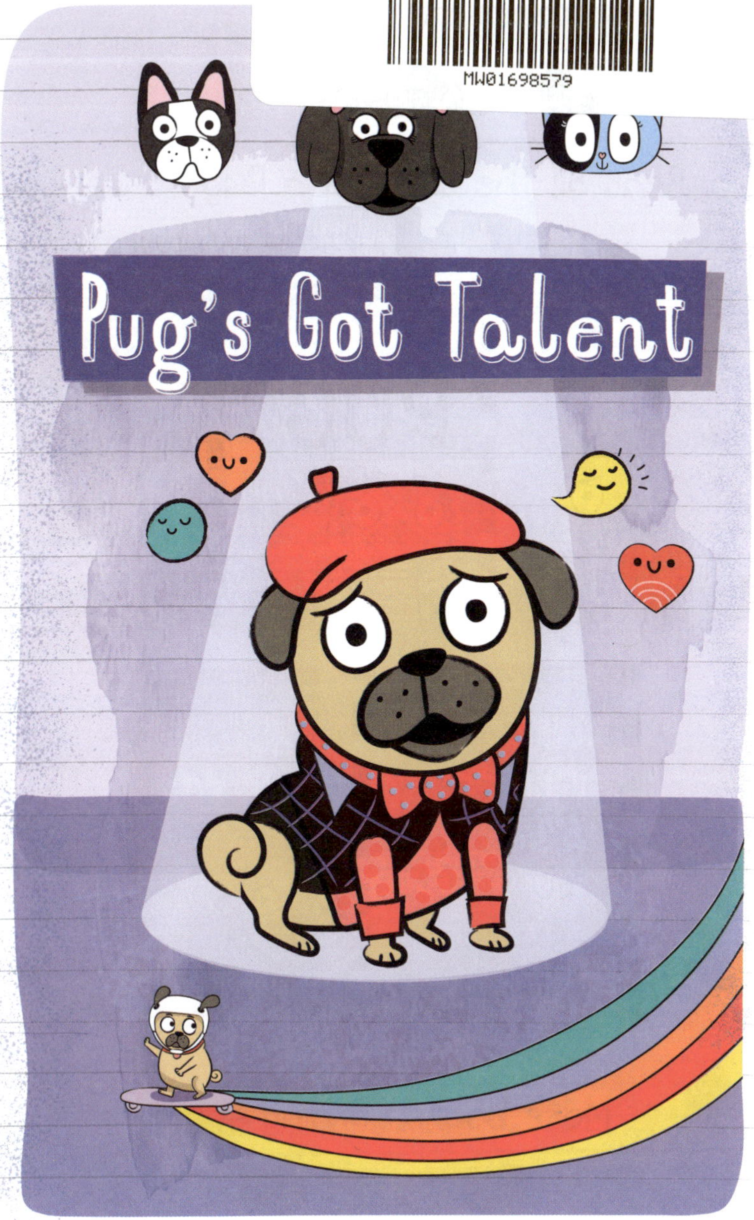
Pug's Got Talent

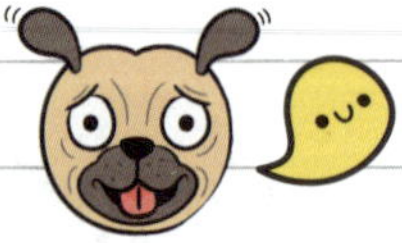

Read all the Diary of a Pug books!

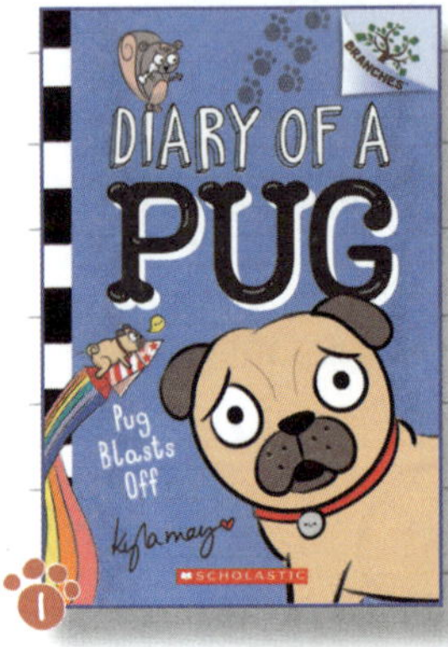

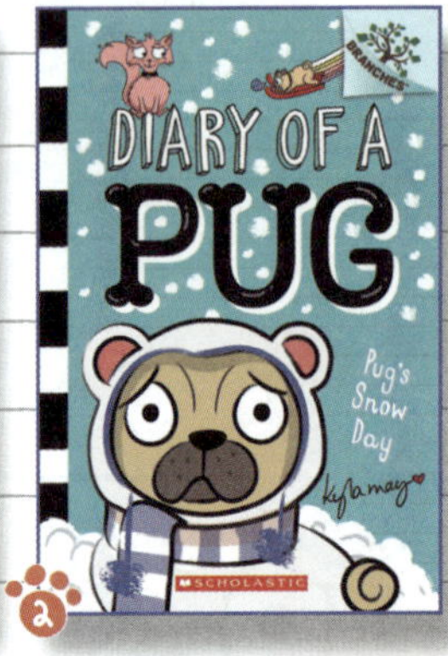

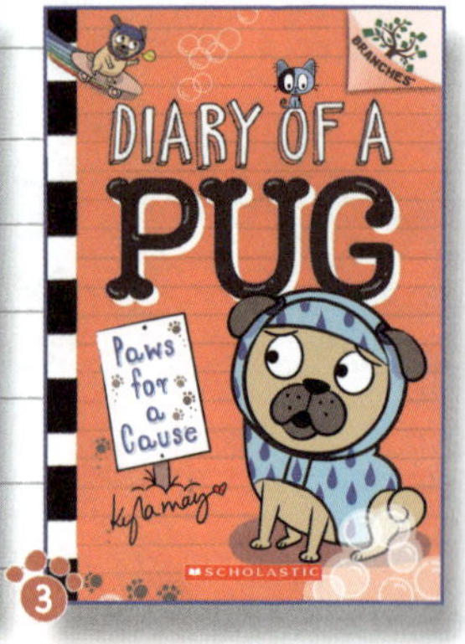

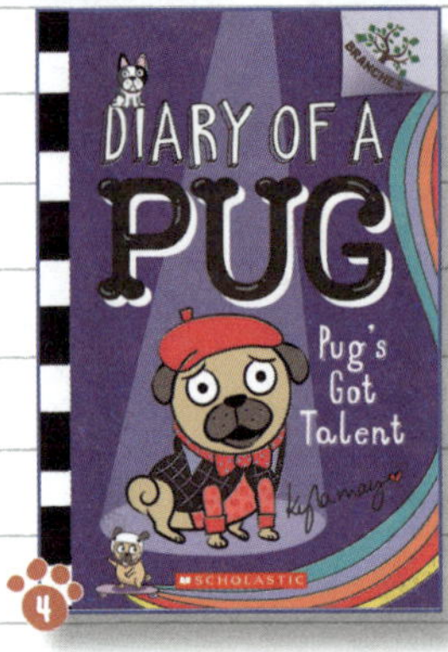

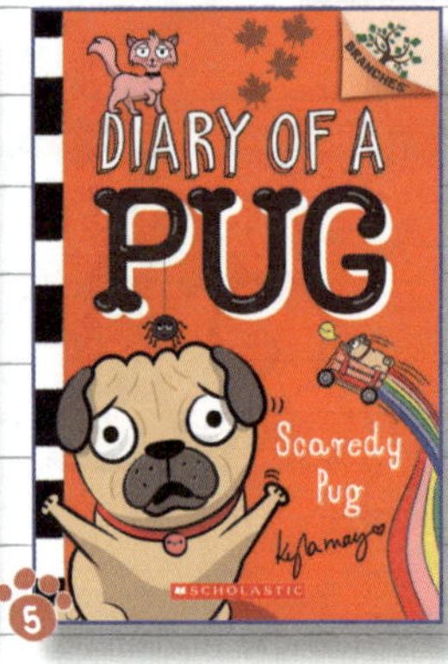

More books coming soon!

DIARY OF A PUG

Pug's Got Talent

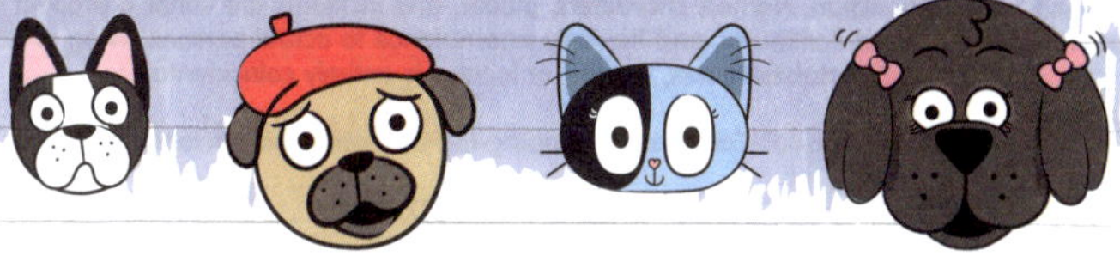

By Kyla May

BRANCHES™

SCHOLASTIC INC.

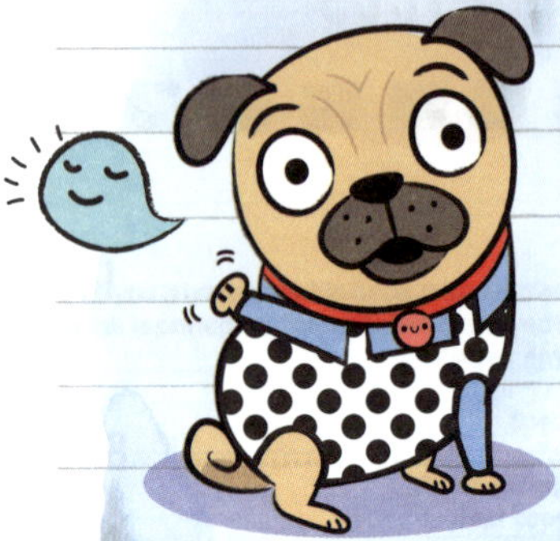

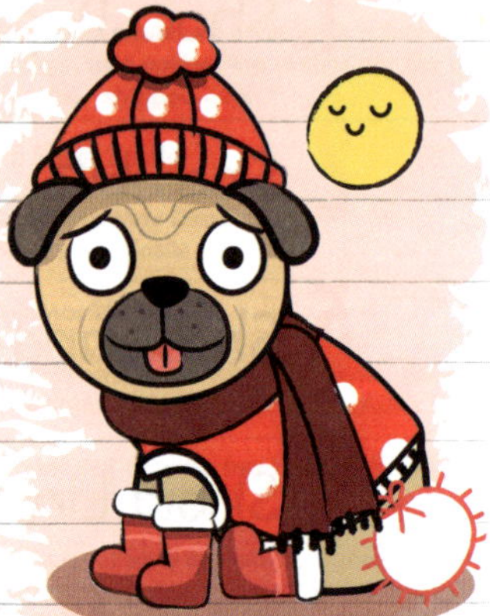

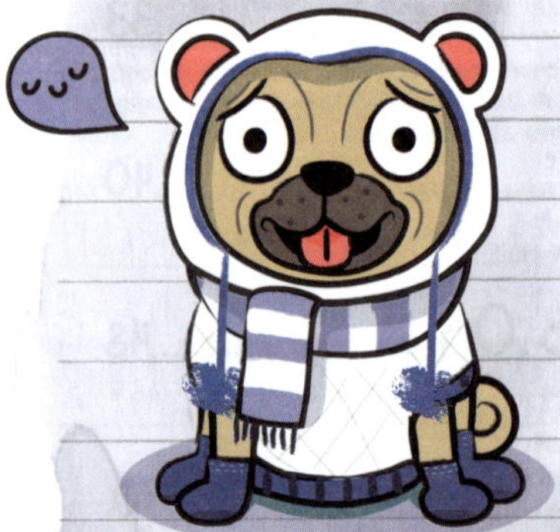

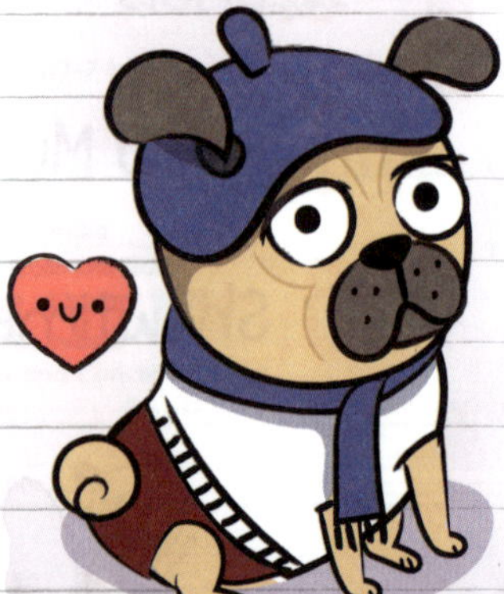

Chapter 1

SHOW DOG

SATURDAY

Dear Diary,

BVB here. That's **BARON VON BUBBLES**. But everyone calls me **BUB.**

Wait until you hear my show-stopping news!

But first, here are some things to know about me:

I have a passion for fashion.

I make many different faces:

Naptime Face

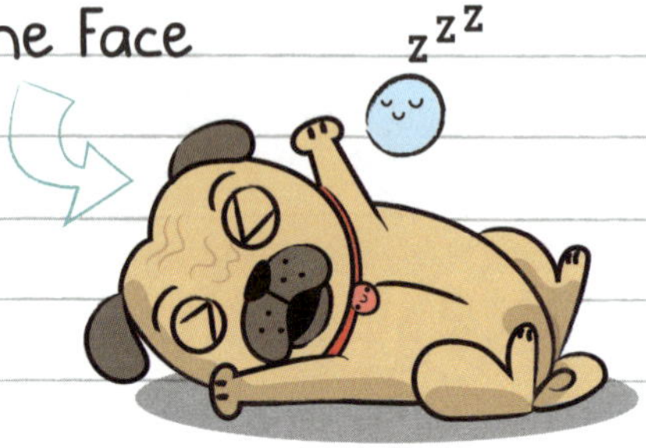

Splashed with Water Face

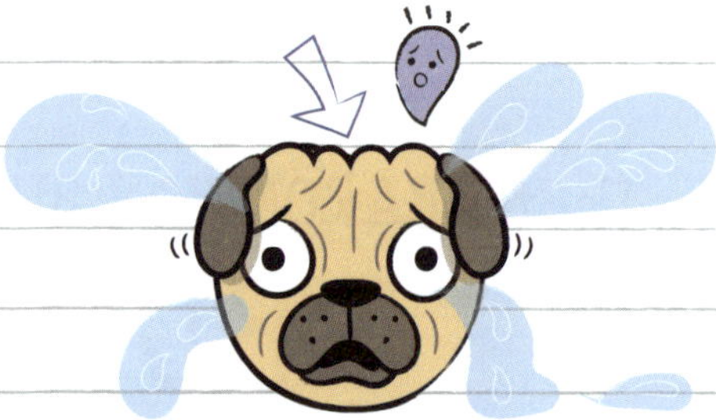

Nervous Face (or I Just Farted Face)

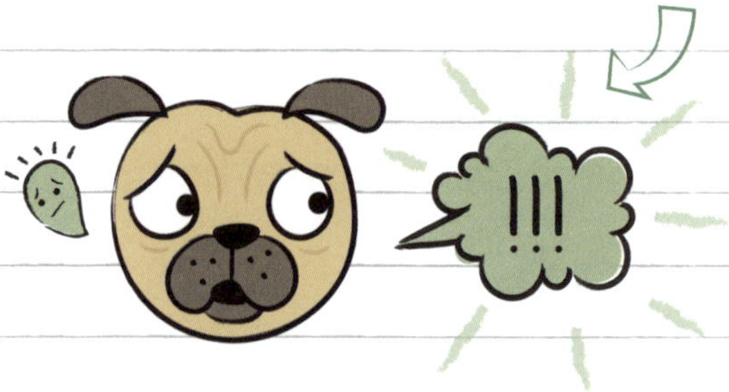

Here are some of my favorite things:

MY SKATEBOARD

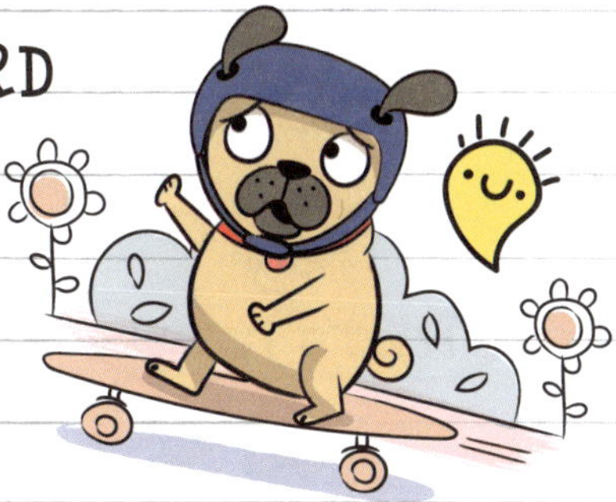

PEANUT BUTTER TREATS

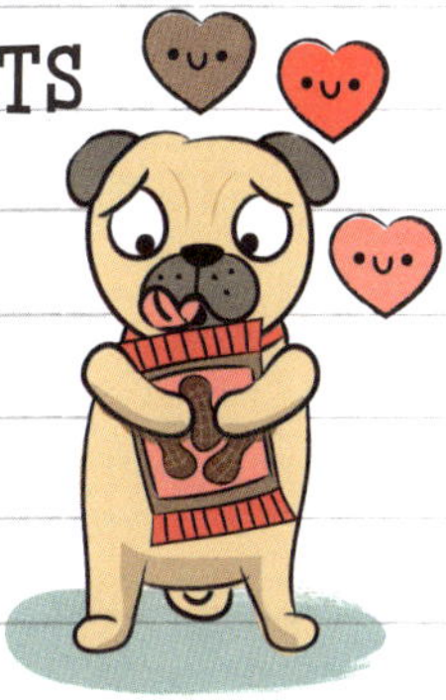

MY BEST FRIEND

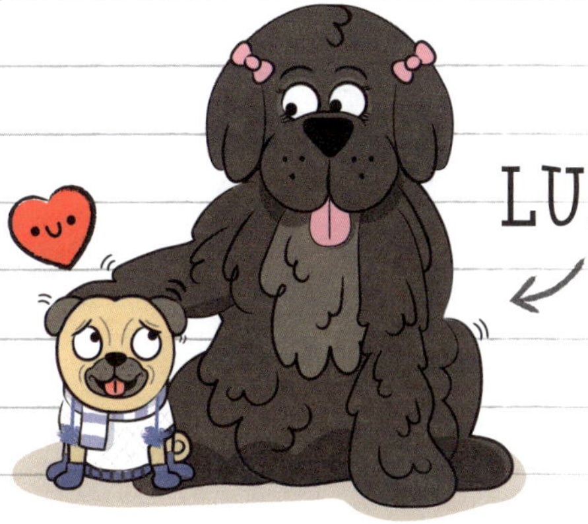

LUNA

Here are some things that get on my nerves:

DUCHESS

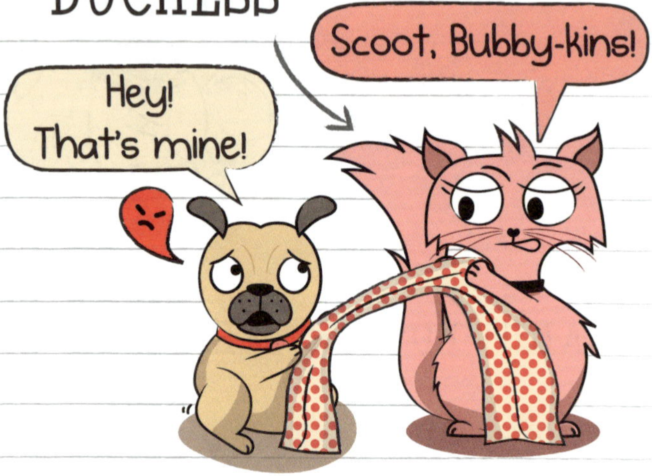

NUTZ

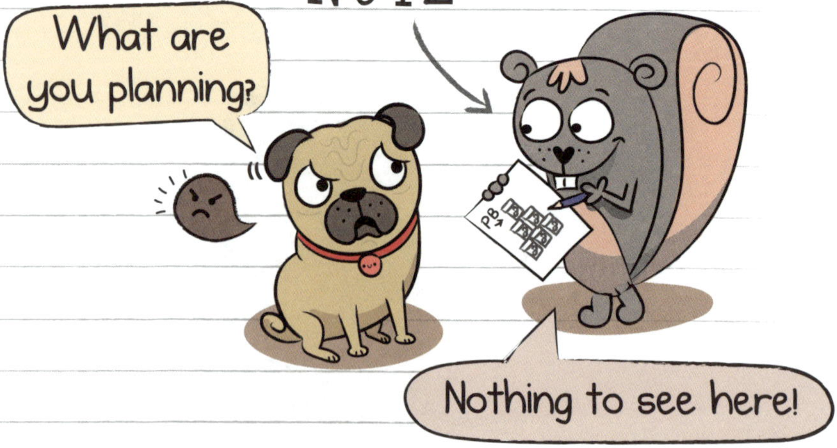

And **WATER**! That's right! I still don't like water!

Bella laughed so hard the first time I jumped into a bubble bath. I had no idea there was WATER under the bubbles! (That's how I got my name, by the way.)

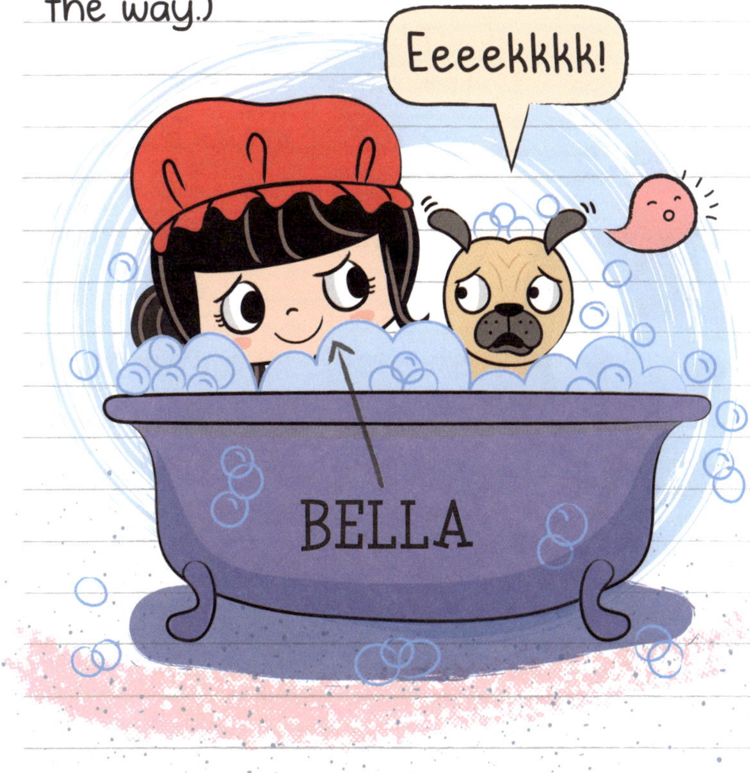

Now back to my show-stopping news! On our walk today, Bella told me about a block party that will take place in front of our house next Saturday.

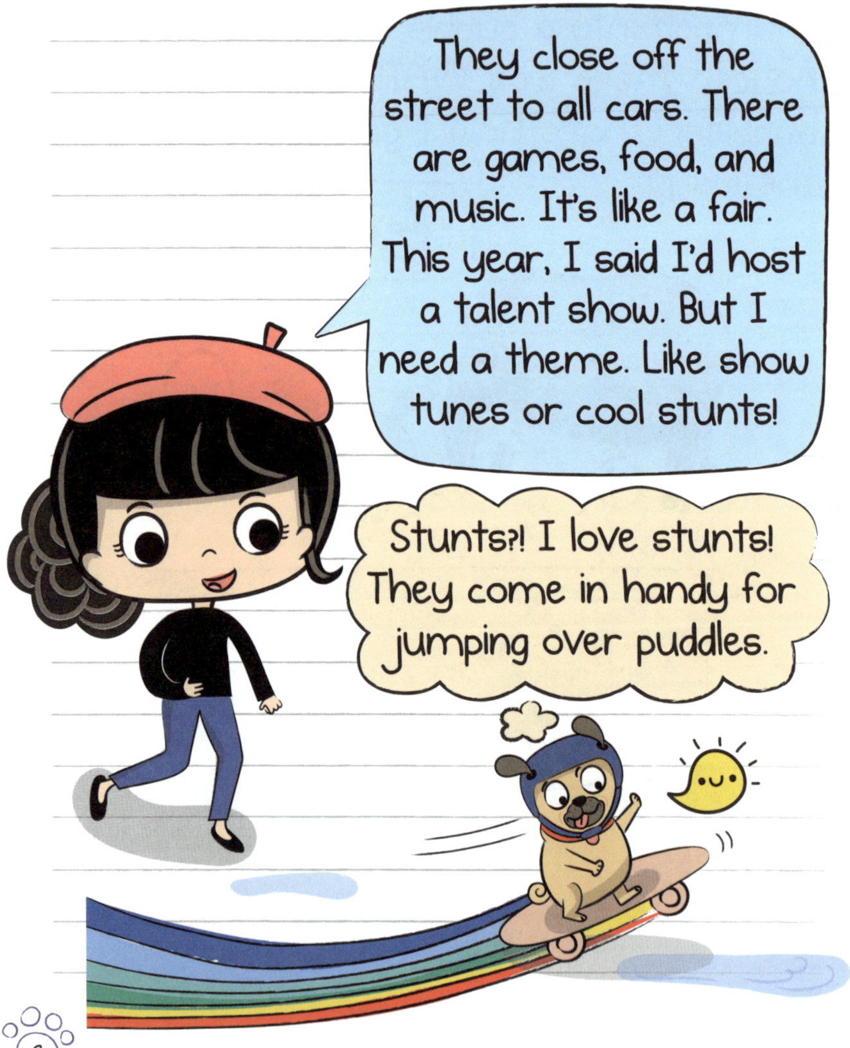

Bella saw my stunt. She stopped and scooped me up.

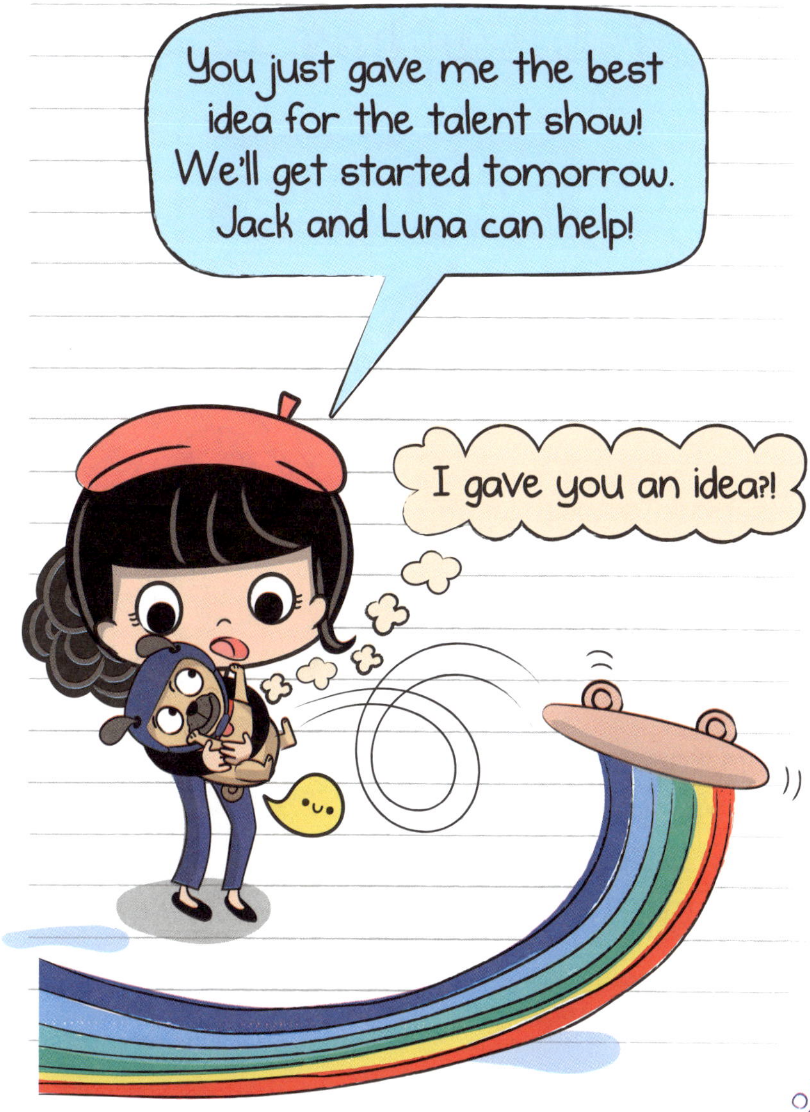

Chapter 2

SHOWBIZ

SUNDAY

Dear Diary,

I had to wait until we were all in Jack and Luna's tree fort to hear Bella's idea.

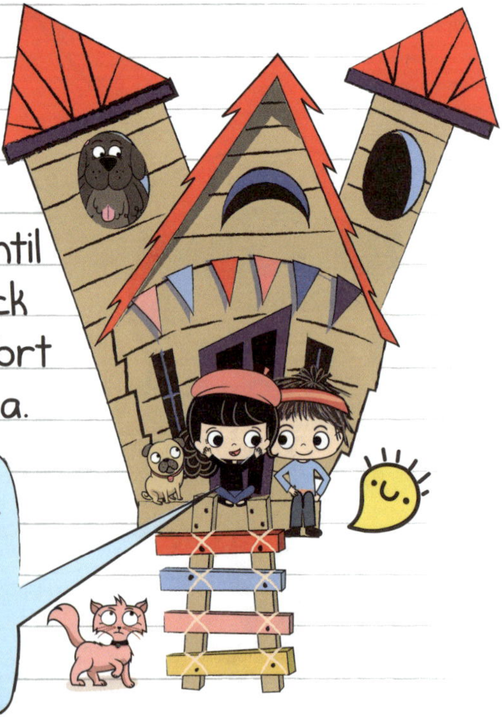

A pet talent show sounded awesome!

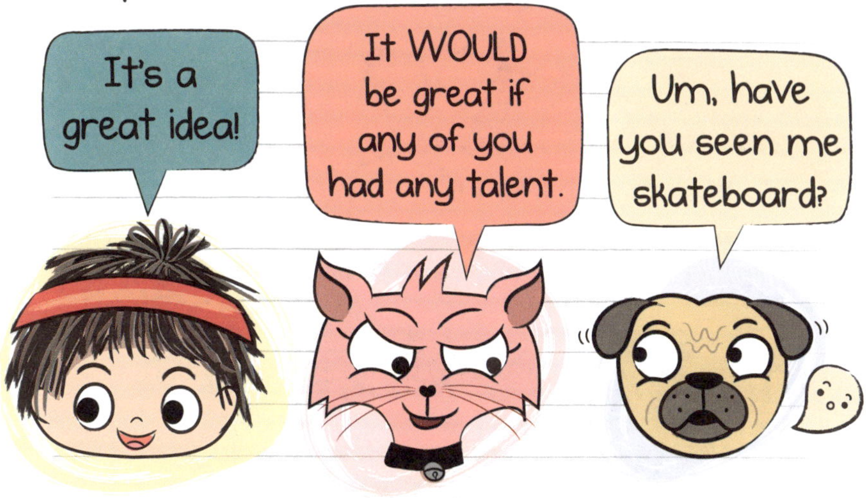

Then Bella said something super exciting.

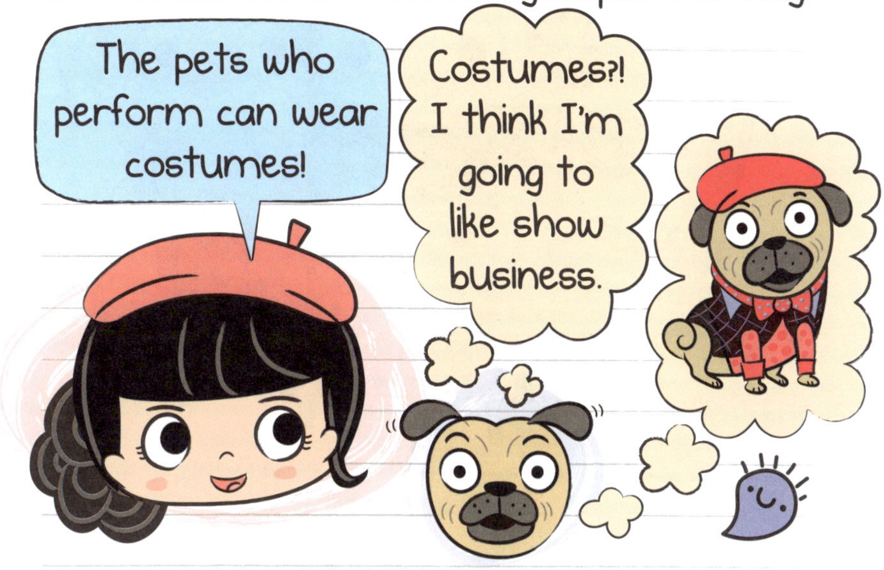

We started planning right away.

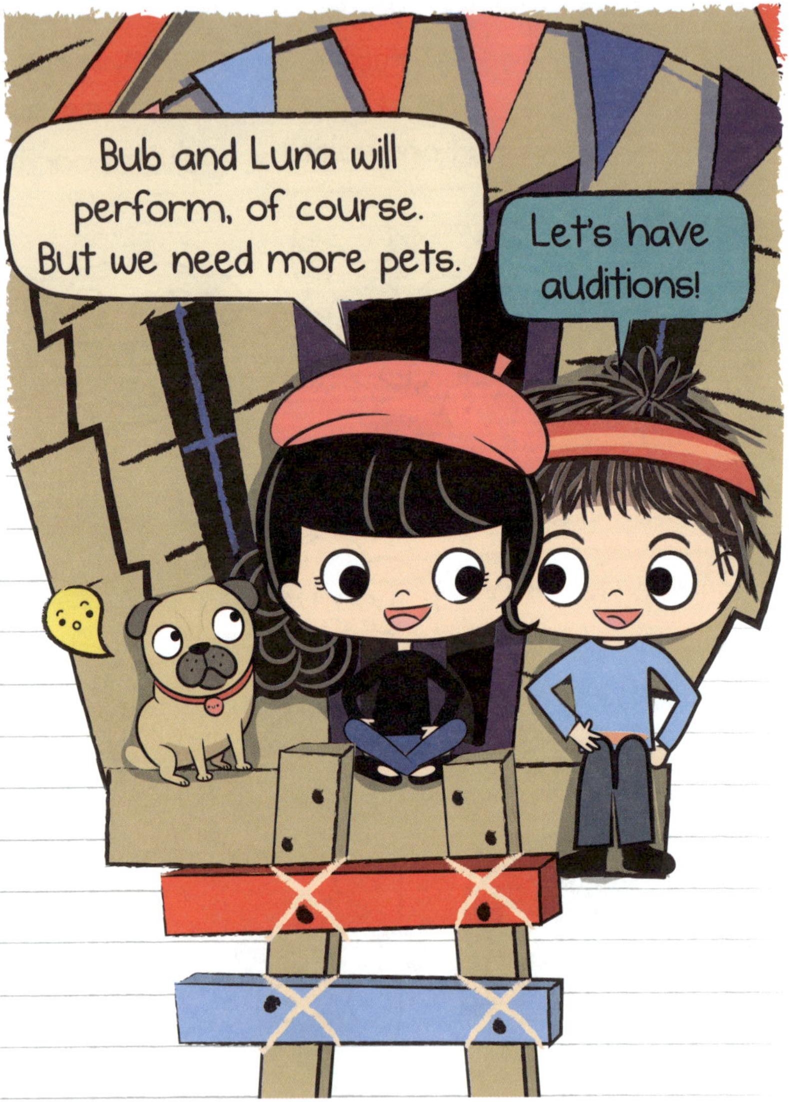

We made flyers. I helped.

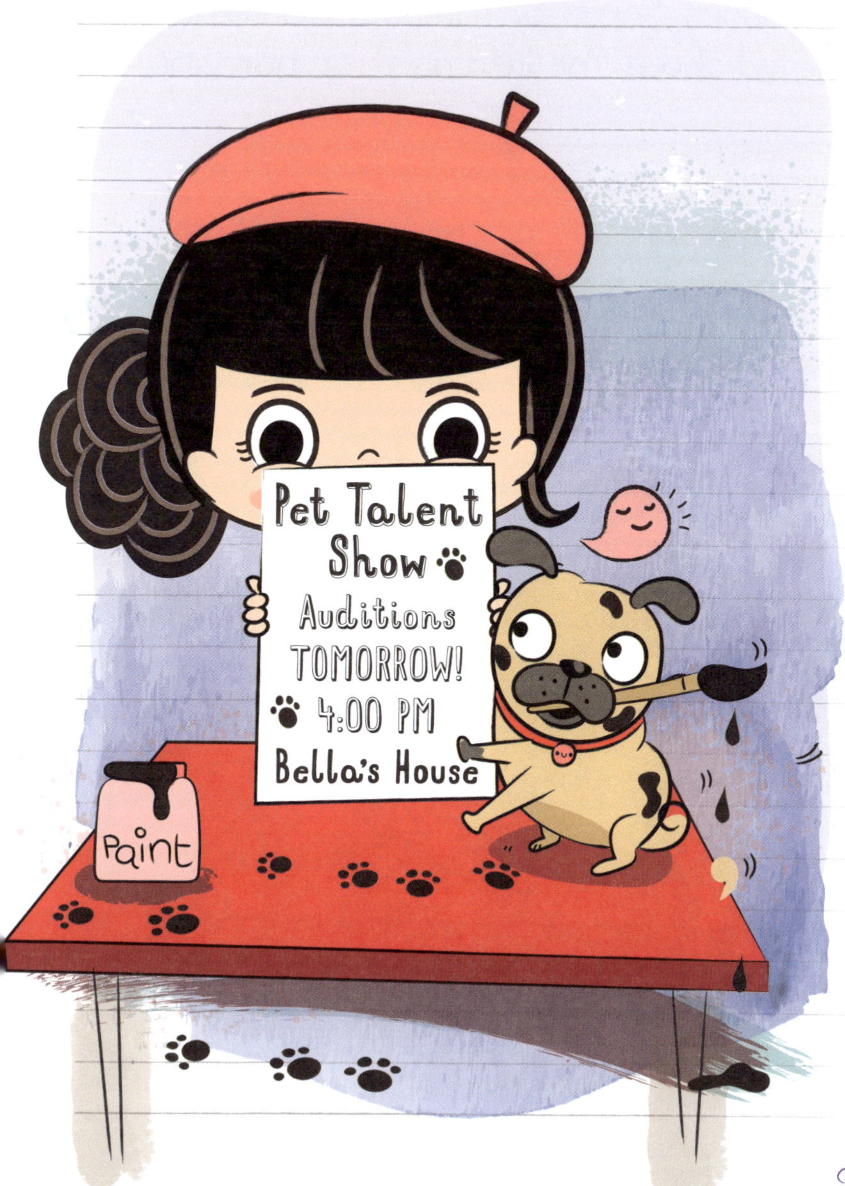

We handed the flyers out to our neighbors. Some of the pets weren't as excited about the idea as their humans.

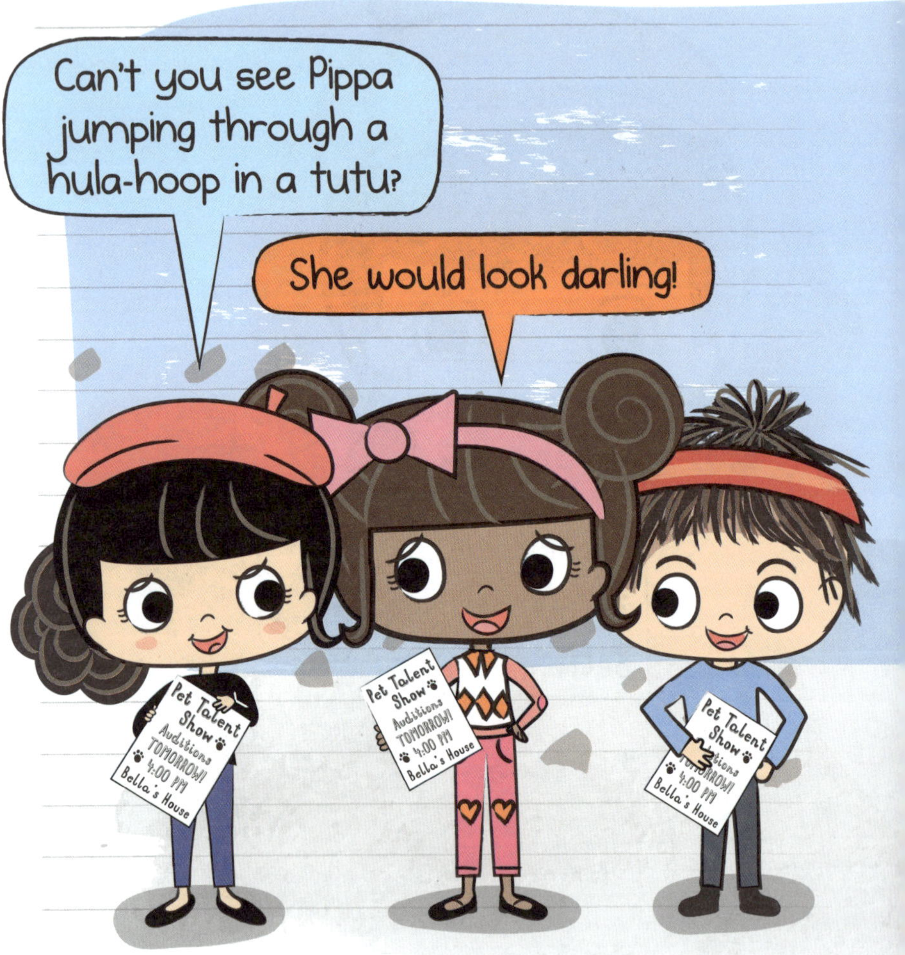

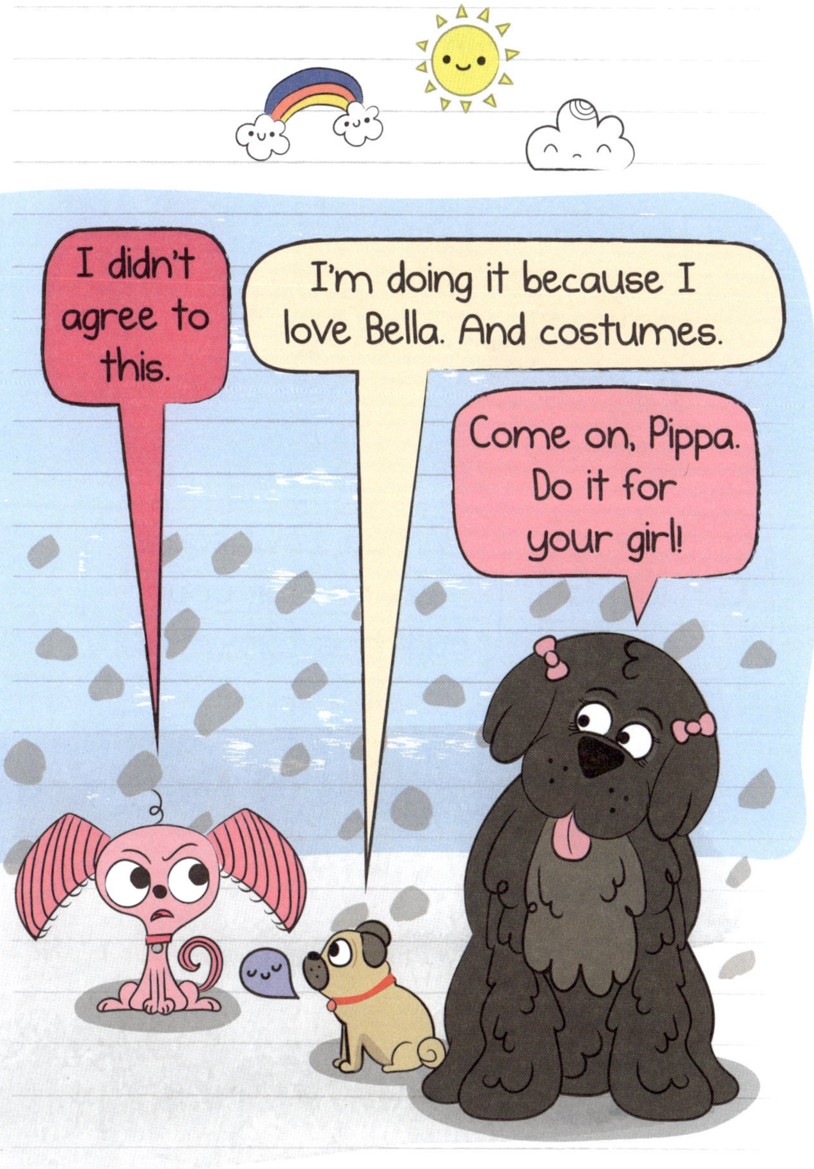
I didn't agree to this.
I'm doing it because I love Bella. And costumes.
Come on, Pippa. Do it for your girl!

Other pets couldn't wait for the auditions!

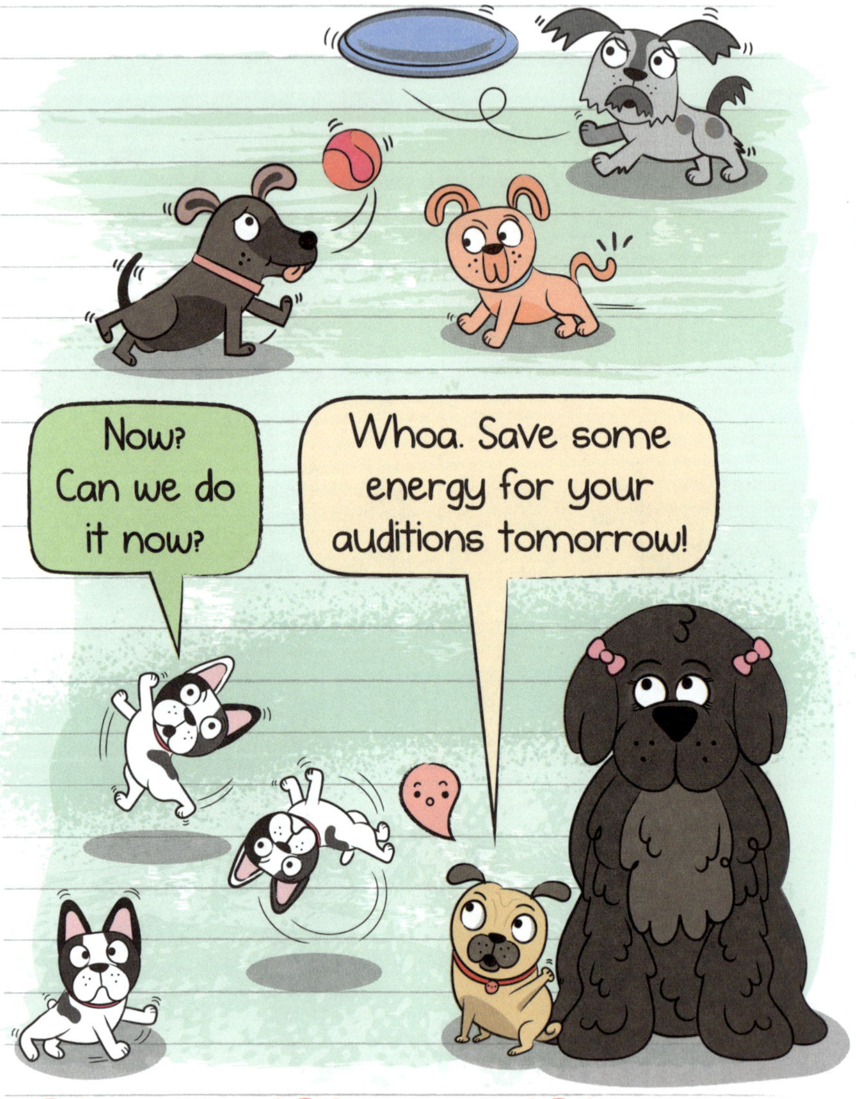

But their humans needed convincing.

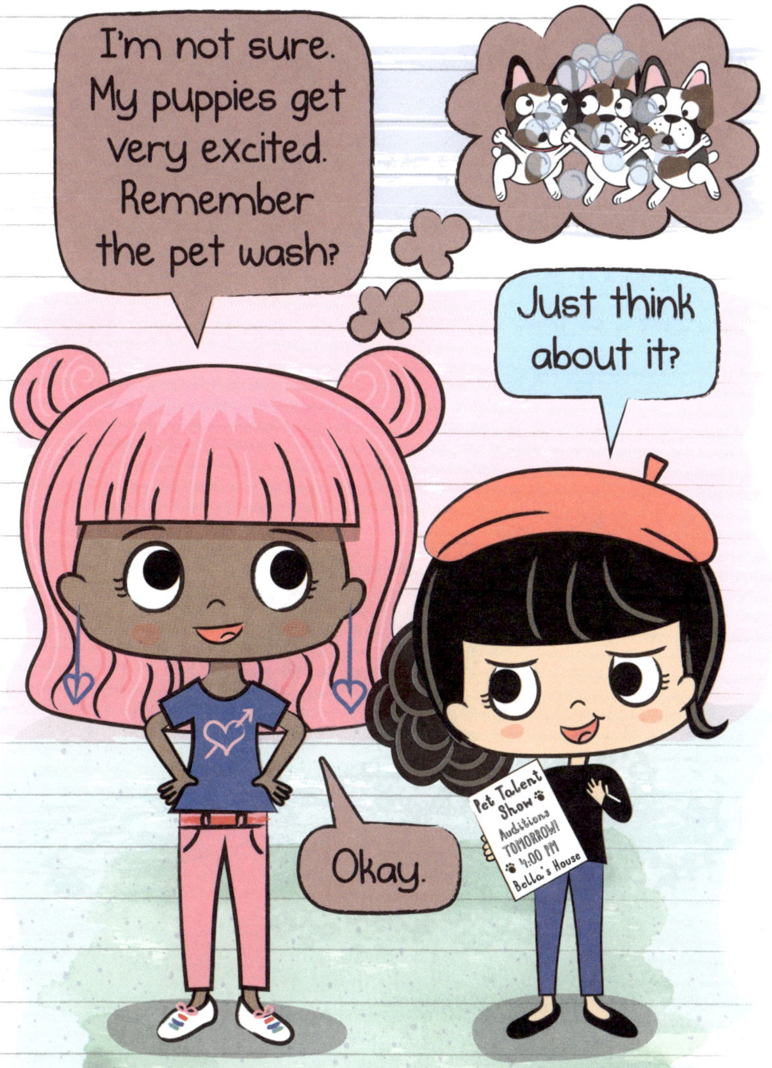

Tonight I was pooped from giving out flyers. But as tired as I was, I couldn't fall asleep. Neither could Bella.

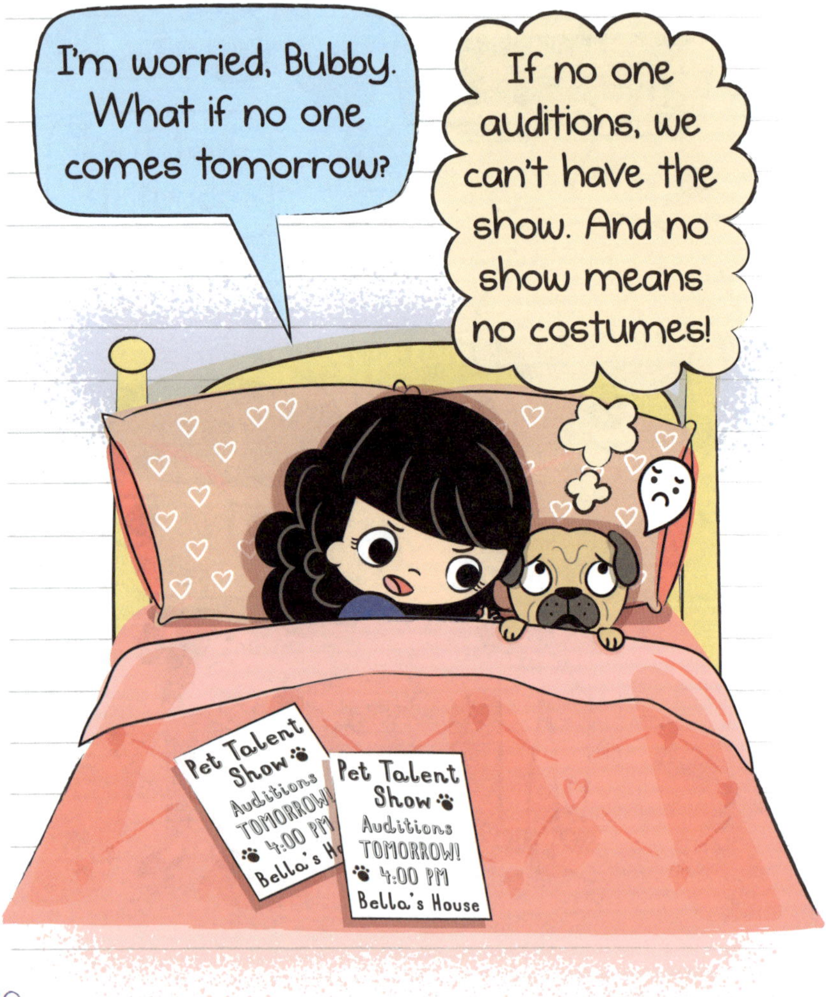

But their humans needed convincing.

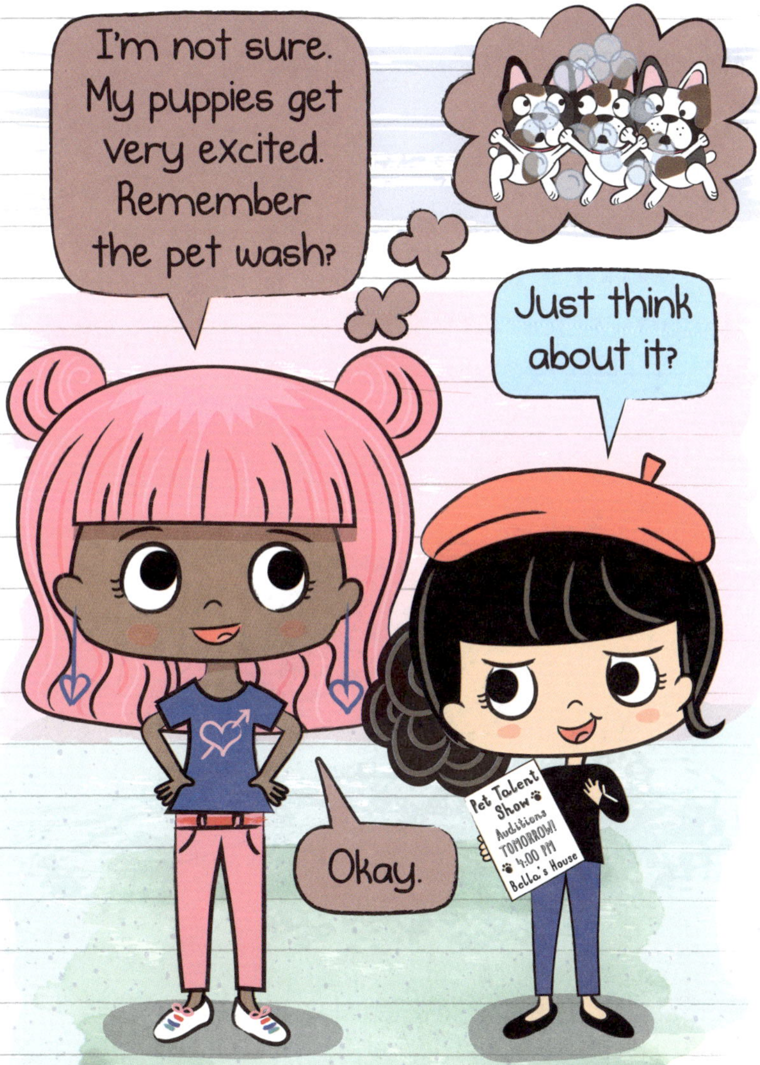

Tonight I was pooped from giving out flyers. But as tired as I was, I couldn't fall asleep. Neither could Bella.

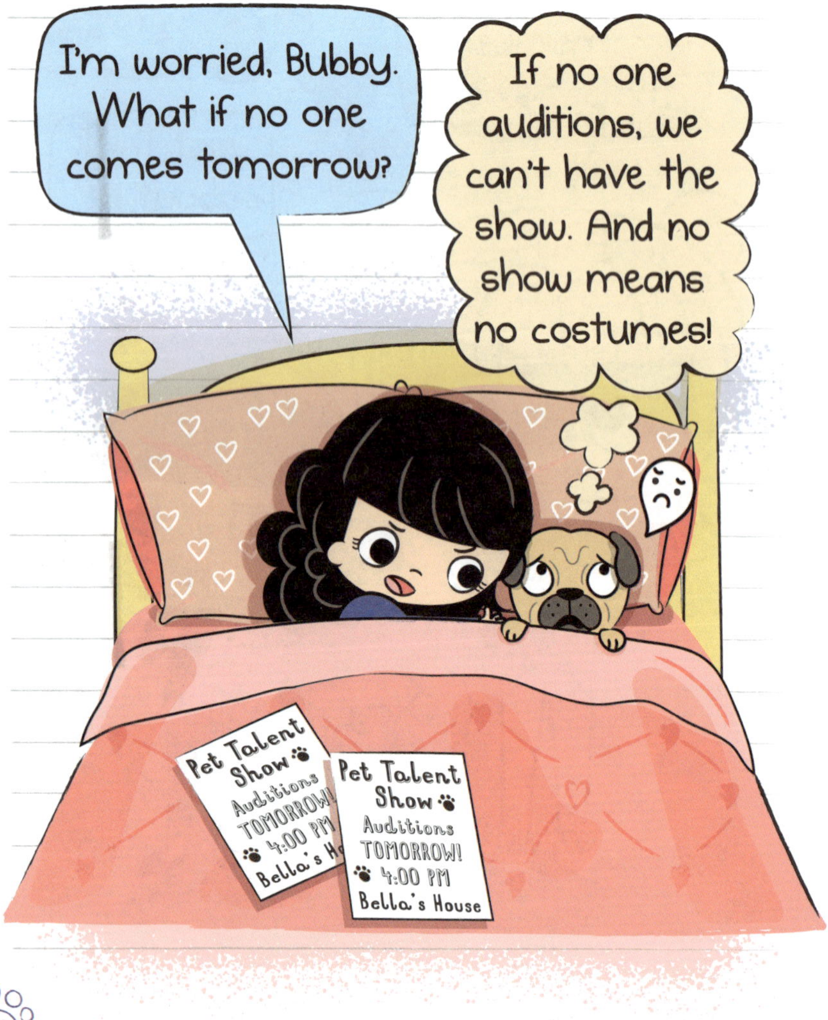

Chapter 3

SHOW AND TELL

MONDAY

Dear Diary,

All four of us were nervous as Jack and Bella headed off to school. Bella tried to lighten the mood by asking about Luna's act.

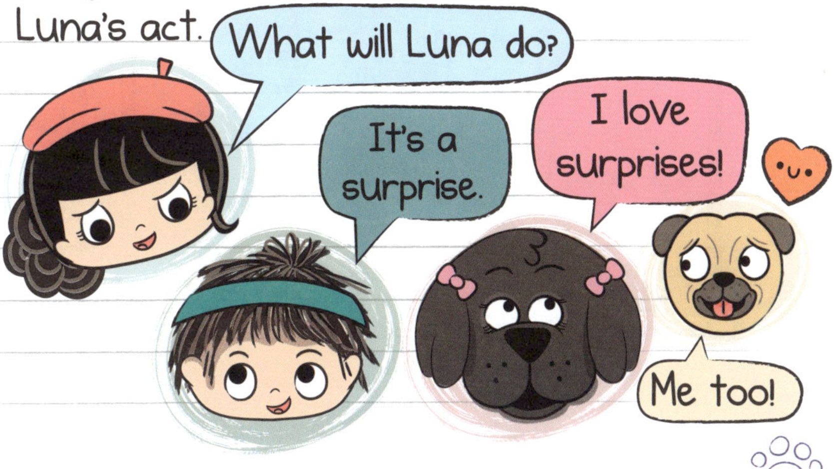

After school, the line of pets waiting to audition was all the way down the block!

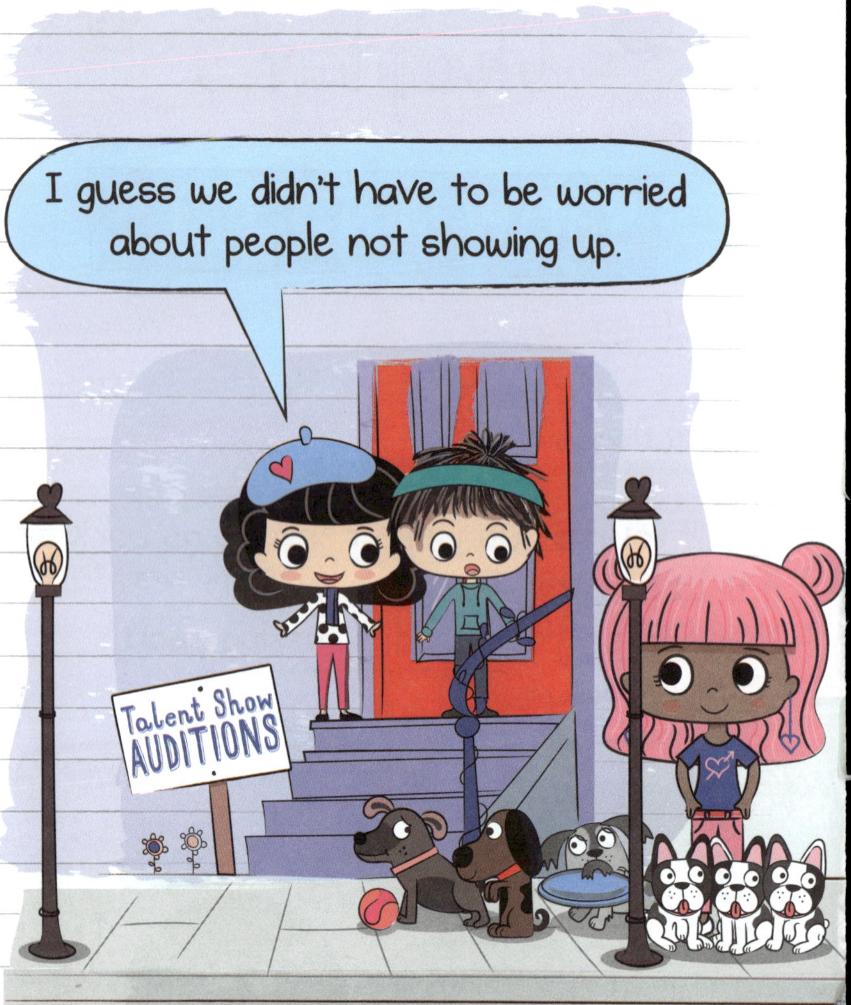

Of course, nosy Nutz had to find out what was going on.

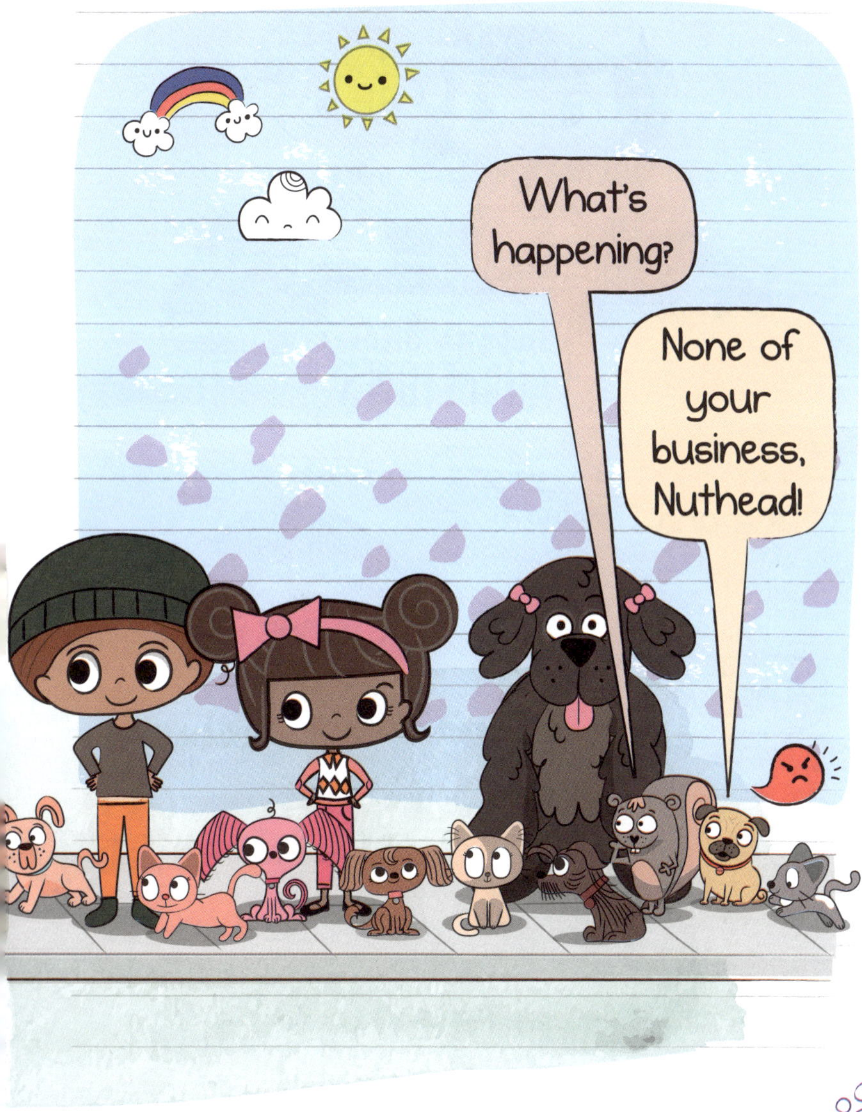

Bella and Jack got the auditions started.

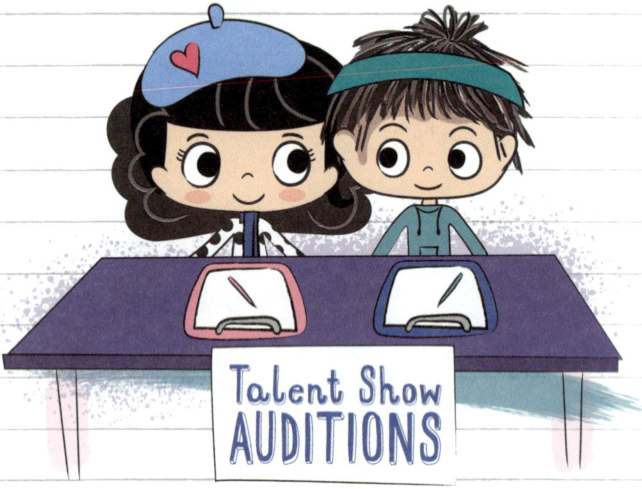

Luna and I helped.

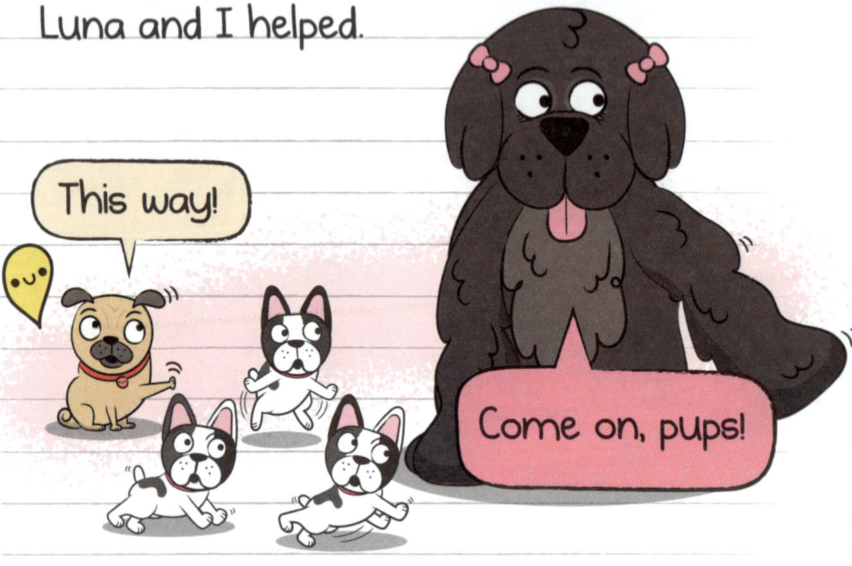

We loved the puppies' act.

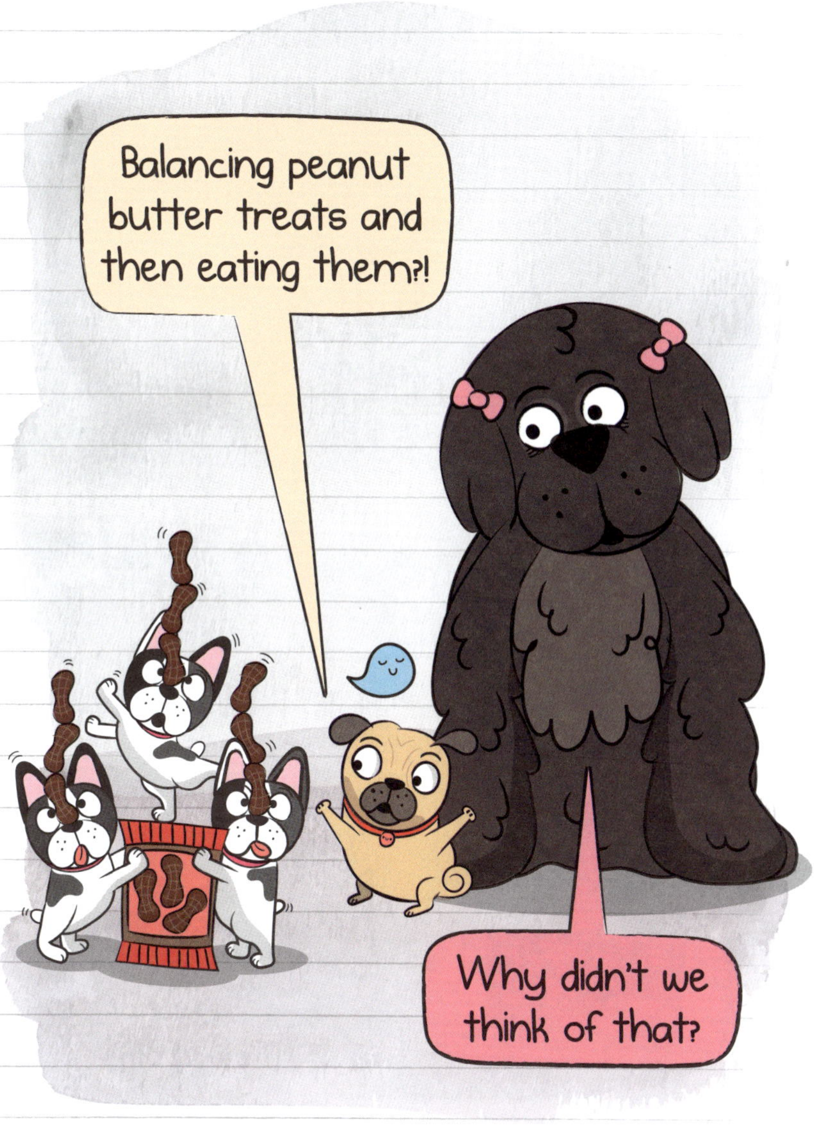

Little Kitty was next. I was impressed by her high-wire act. Duchess wasn't.

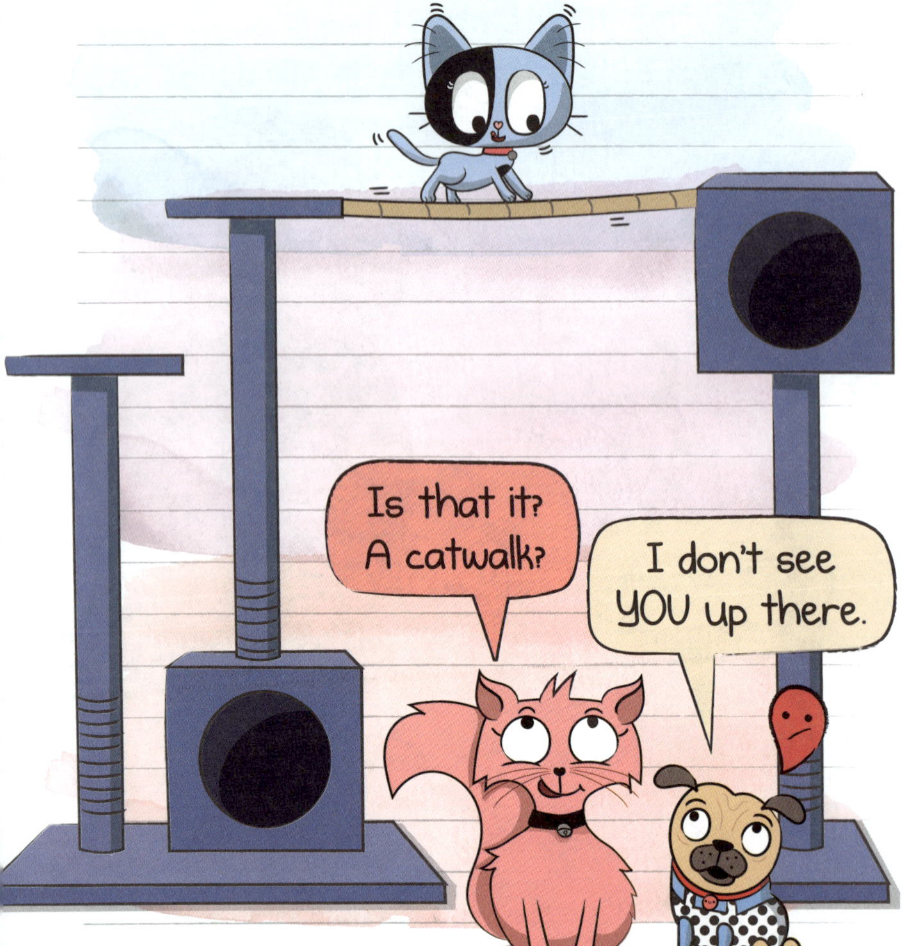

A few acts didn't go well.

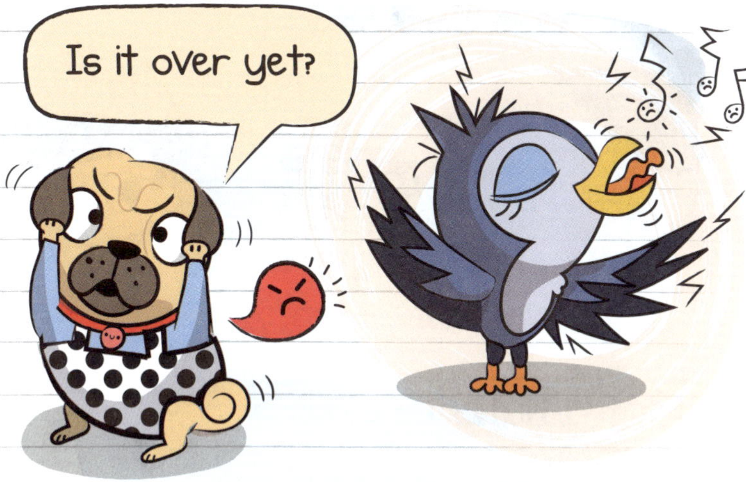

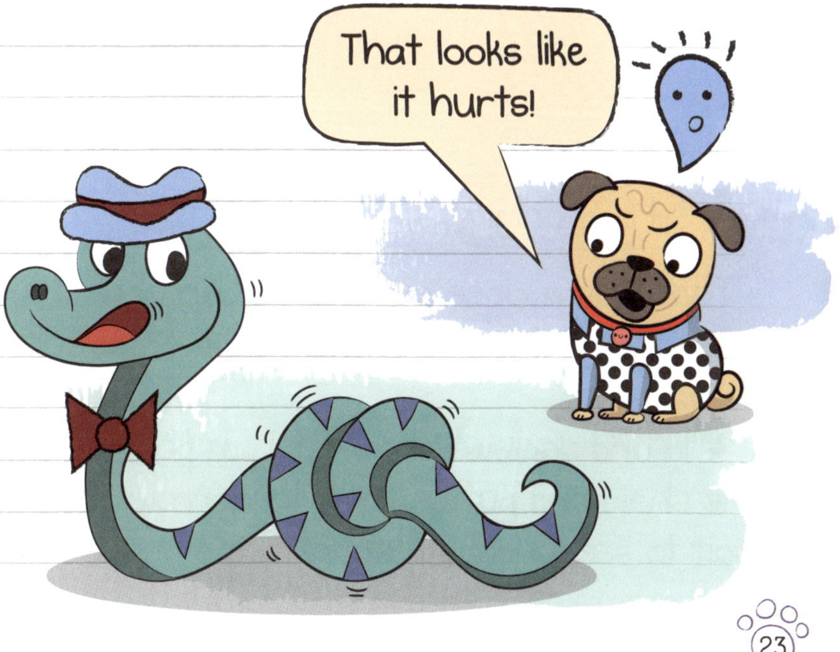

Then guess what happened, Diary? Nutz tried to get in the show!

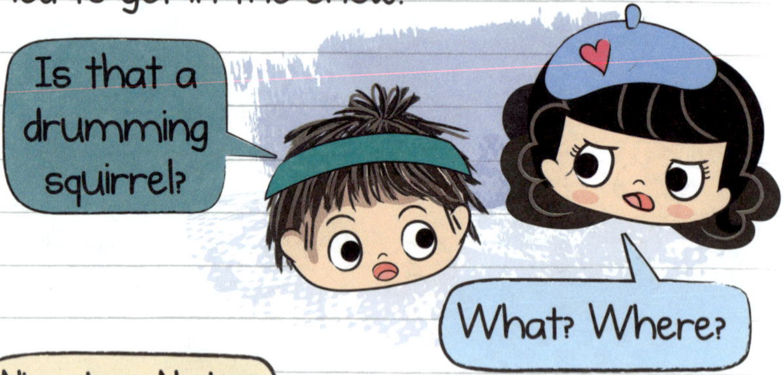

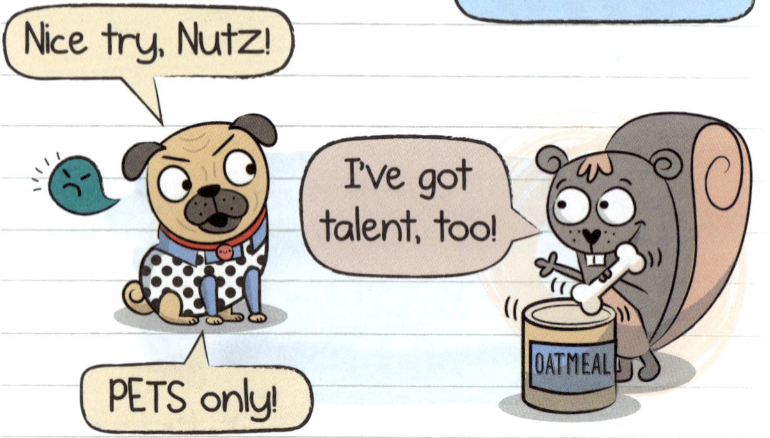

That was a close one, Diary. Can you imagine the trouble he would have caused?!

Bella and Jack will choose which pets will be in the show and put up a list tomorrow. I can't wait to see who I will share the stage with!

Chapter 4

SHOW LINEUP

TUESDAY

Dear Diary,

Bella and I got up early to hang up the list of acts.

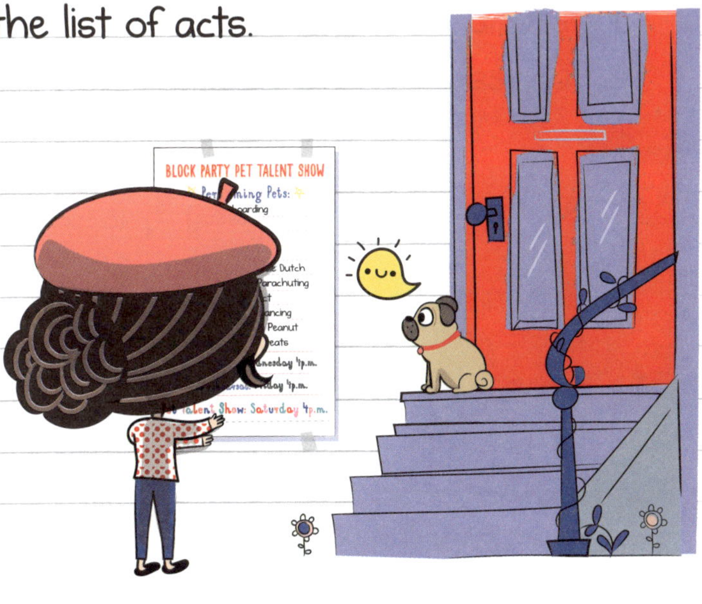

BLOCK PARTY PET TALENT SHOW

Performing Pets:

1. Bub: Skateboarding
2. Pippa: Hula-Hoop
3. Kitty: High-Wire
4. Bitty Birds: Flying
5. Border Collie: Double Dutch
6. Gilly Guinea Pig: Parachuting
7. Luna: Surprise Act
8. Petunia Pig: Tap Dancing
9. Puppies: Balancing Peanut Butter Treats

First rehearsal: Wednesday 4p.m.

Dress rehearsal: Friday 4p.m.

Pet Talent Show: Saturday 4p.m.

As Bella and Jack headed to school, they reminded us to practice our acts.

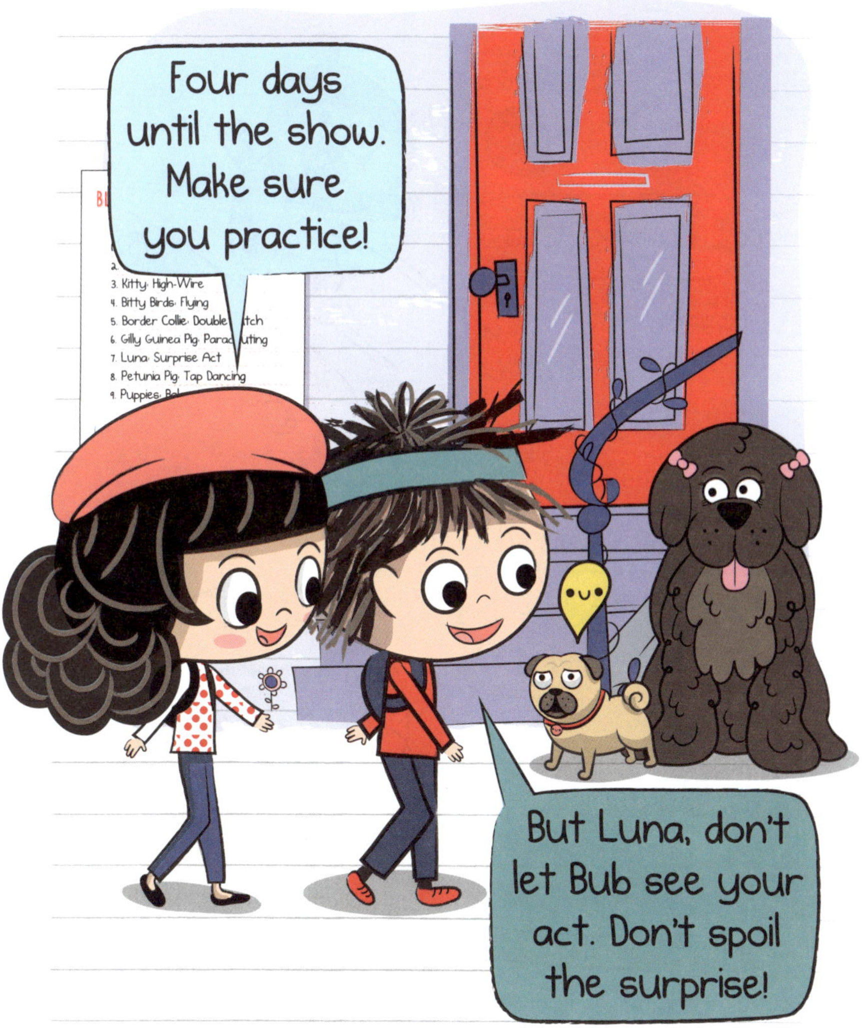

It's driving me crazy not knowing what Luna's act is. Practicing my stunts helped me forget for awhile.

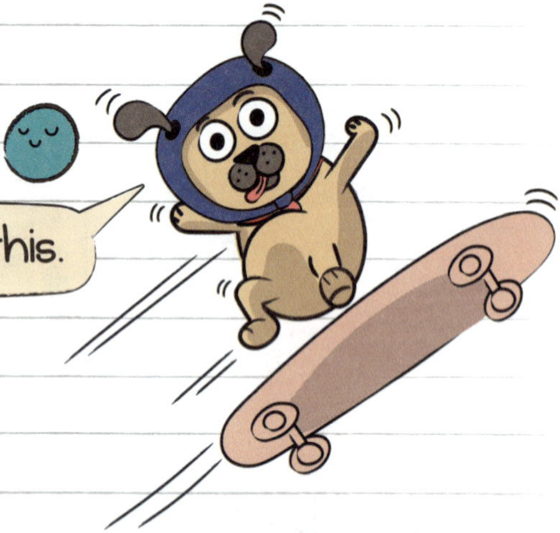

Then Duchess showed up.

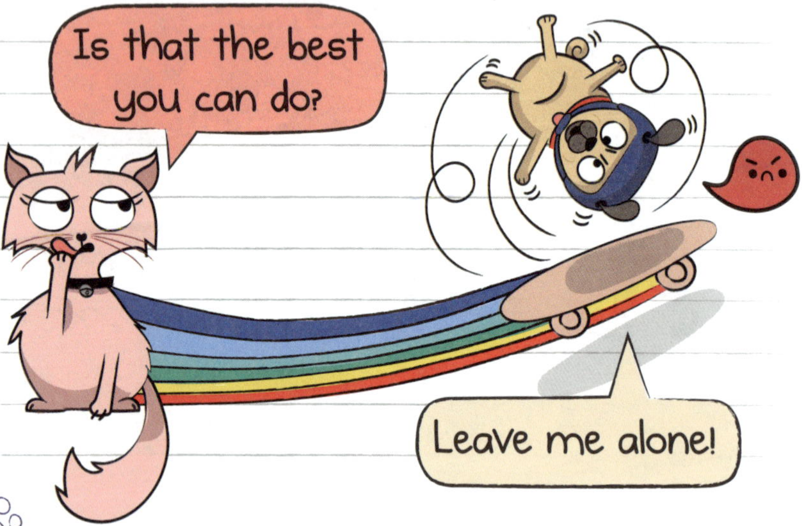

But Duchess never leaves me alone. She pointed out every wrong move I made.

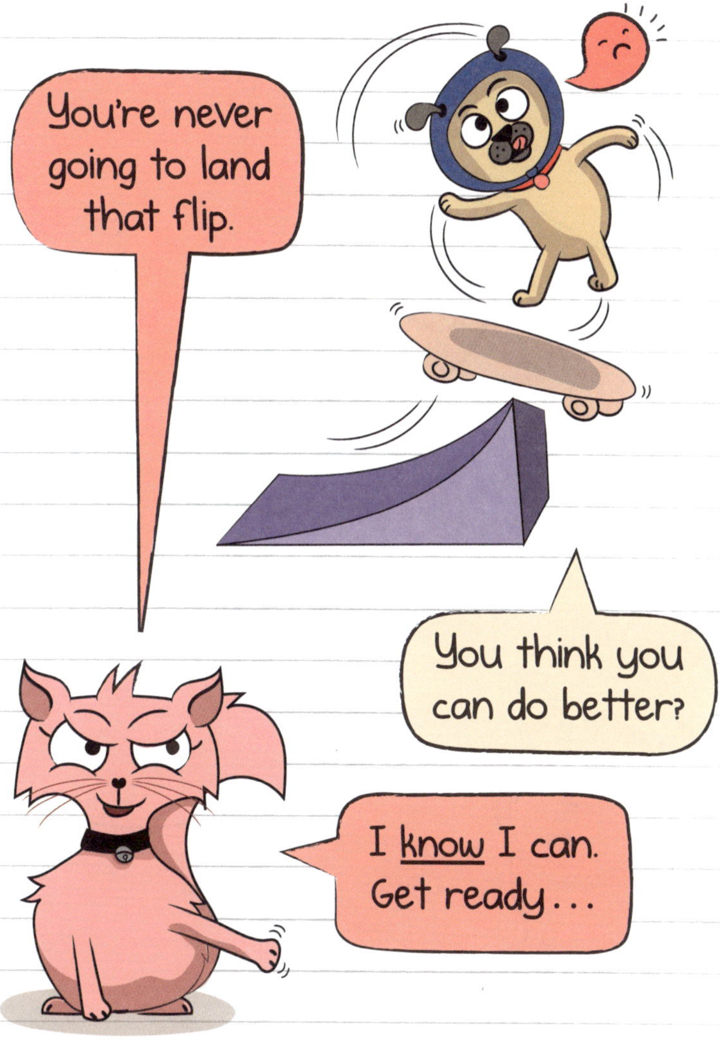

Diary, you won't believe this. Duchess nailed the flip.

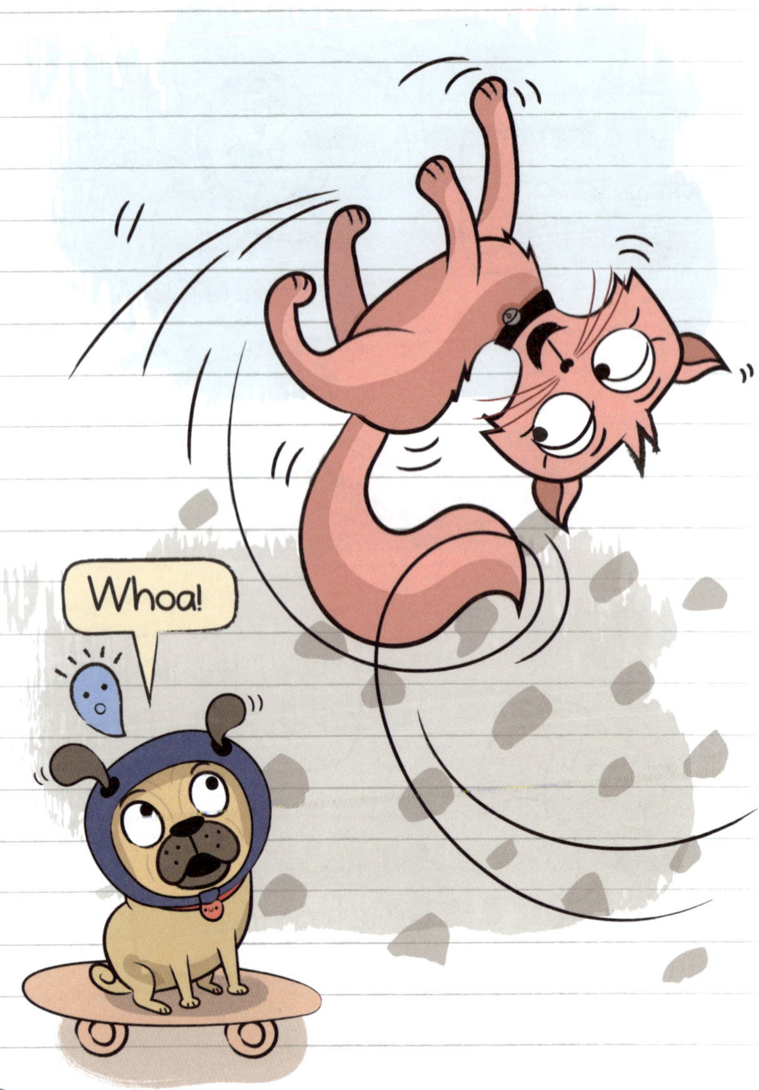

I couldn't believe Duchess was so good at acrobatics.

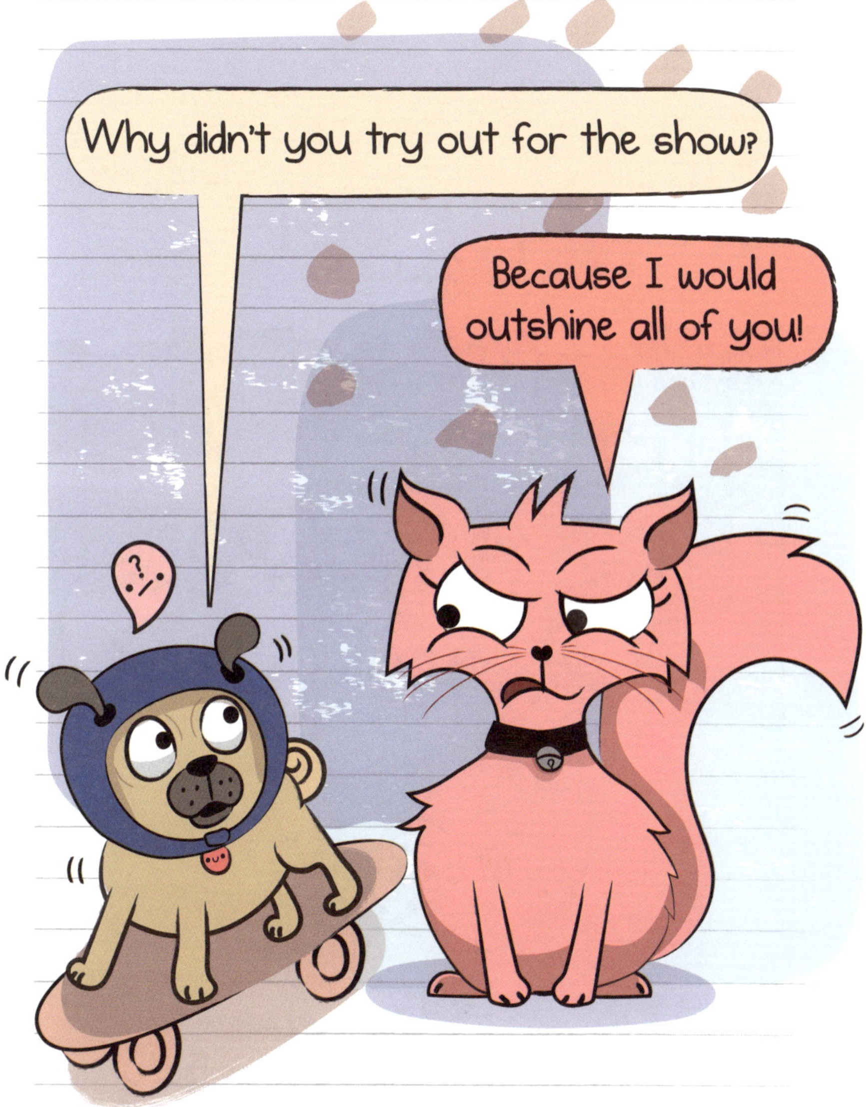

As Duchess proudly marched away, I heard a sound from Luna's backyard.

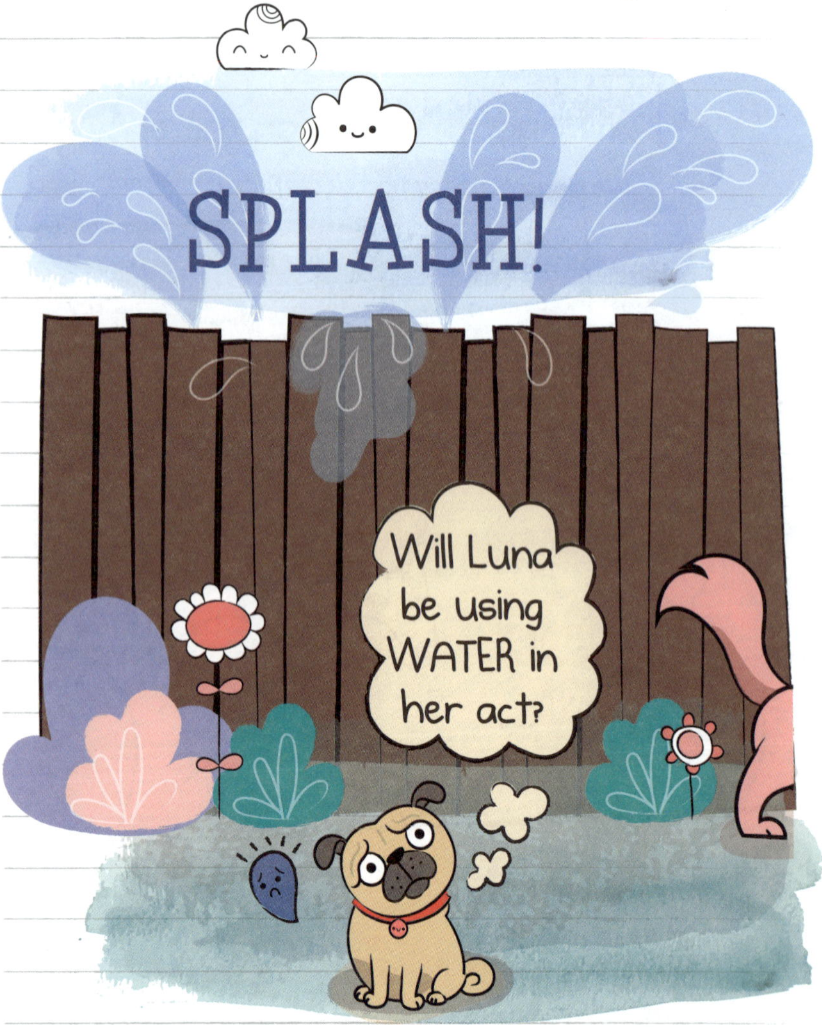

I have a bad feeling about this, Diary!

I rushed out of the splash zone and under the stage just in time. Guess who was hiding under there?

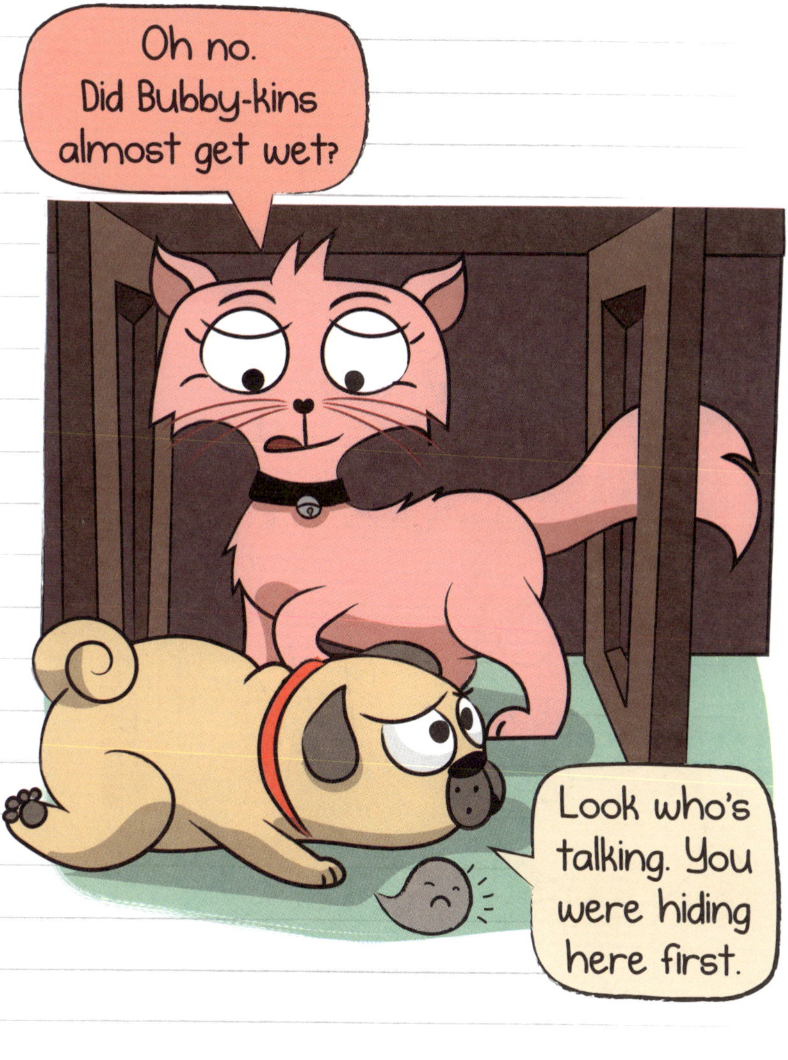

Then it hit me. For not wanting to be in the show, Duchess was hanging around A LOT. I wanted some answers.

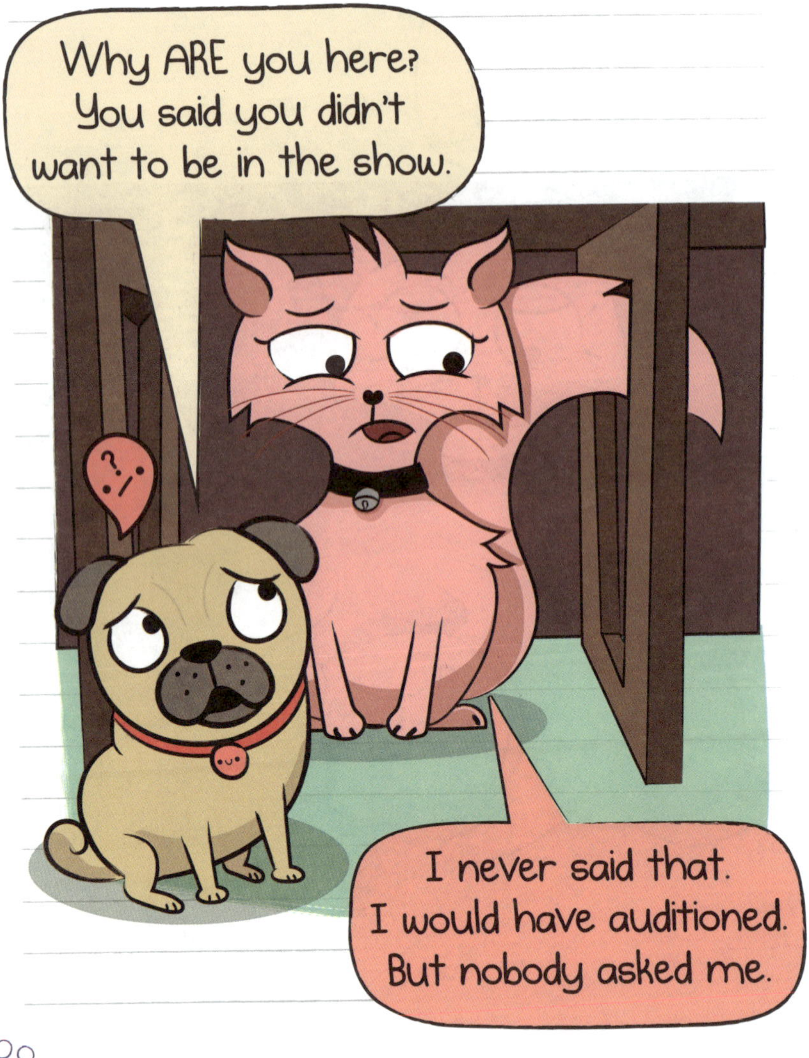

I know it's hard to believe, but Duchess has feelings! And her feelings were hurt.

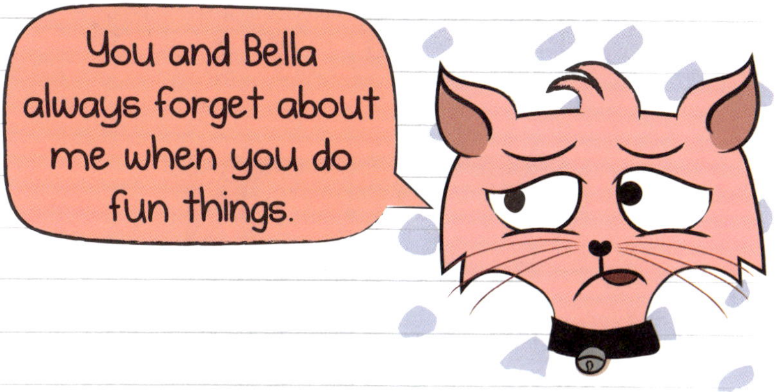

That was true, Diary. We often did things without Duchess.

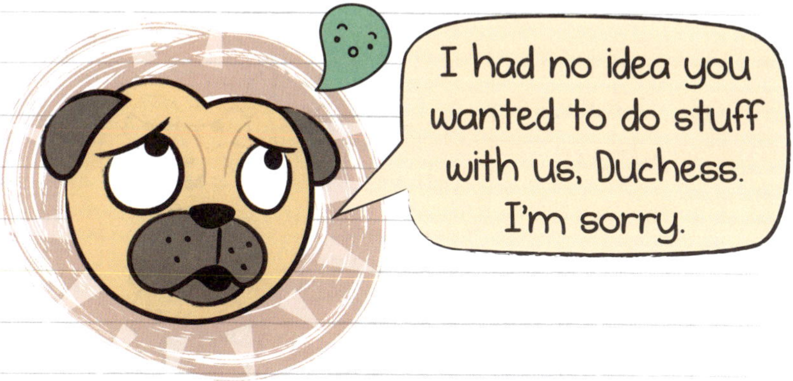

I never thought I'd say this, but I would like to help Duchess. Maybe I can get her in the show. I will make a plan tomorrow.

Chapter 6

SHOW-OFF

THURSDAY

Dear Diary,

This morning, I made a plan to get Duchess in the show. But helping her wasn't easy! We are NOT used to being nice to each other.

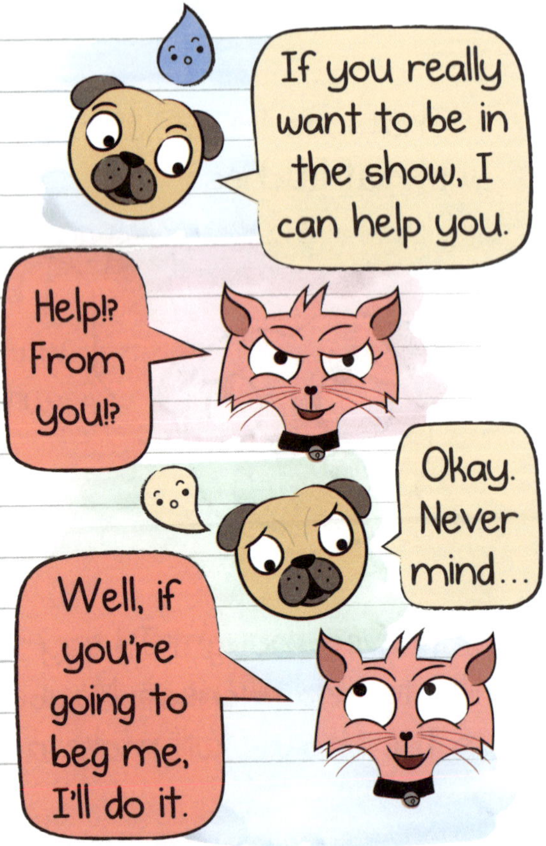

As Bella headed to school, I put my plan into action. Duchess would be in my act with me. I started to show her where she could jump in.

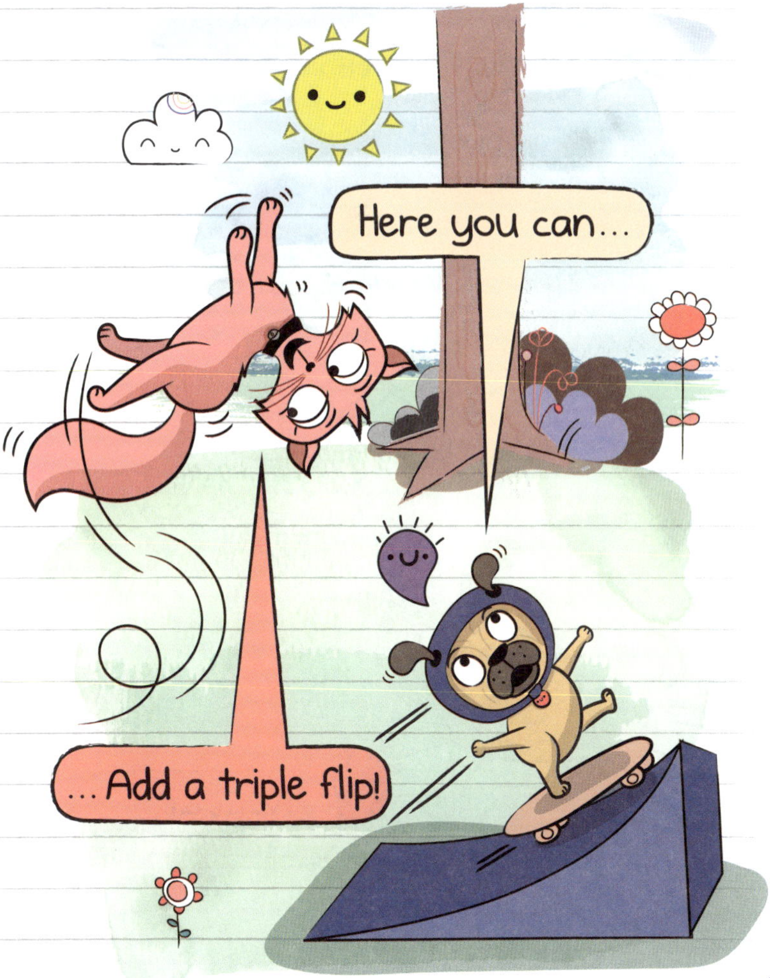

It turned out Duchess already knew my whole act! She had a few ideas of her own.

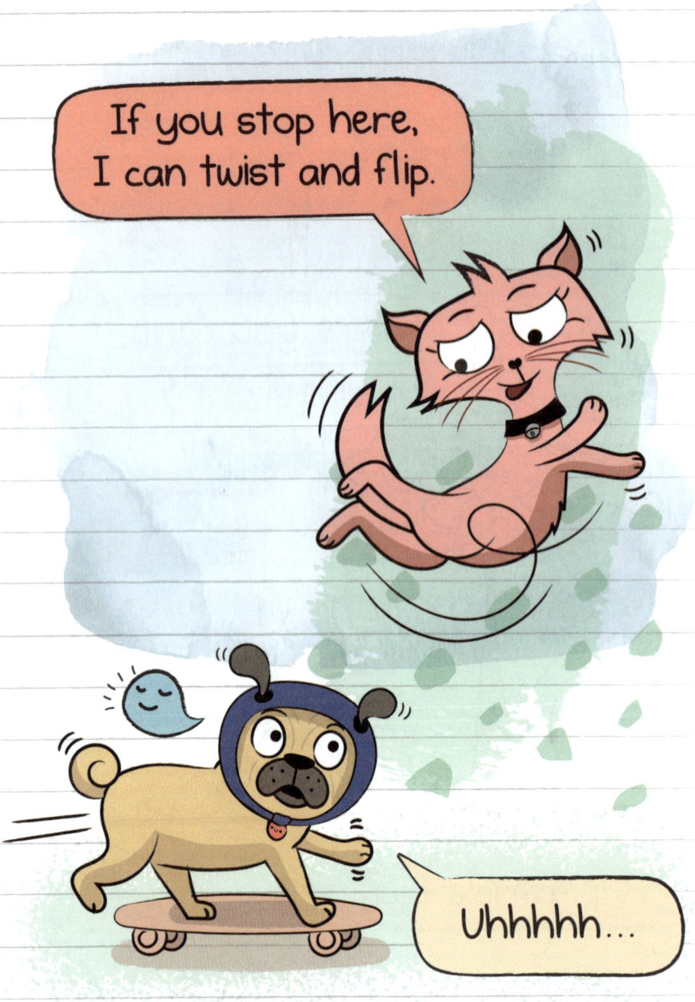

Duchess's ideas were good, but it started to feel like Duchess was the star of MY act.

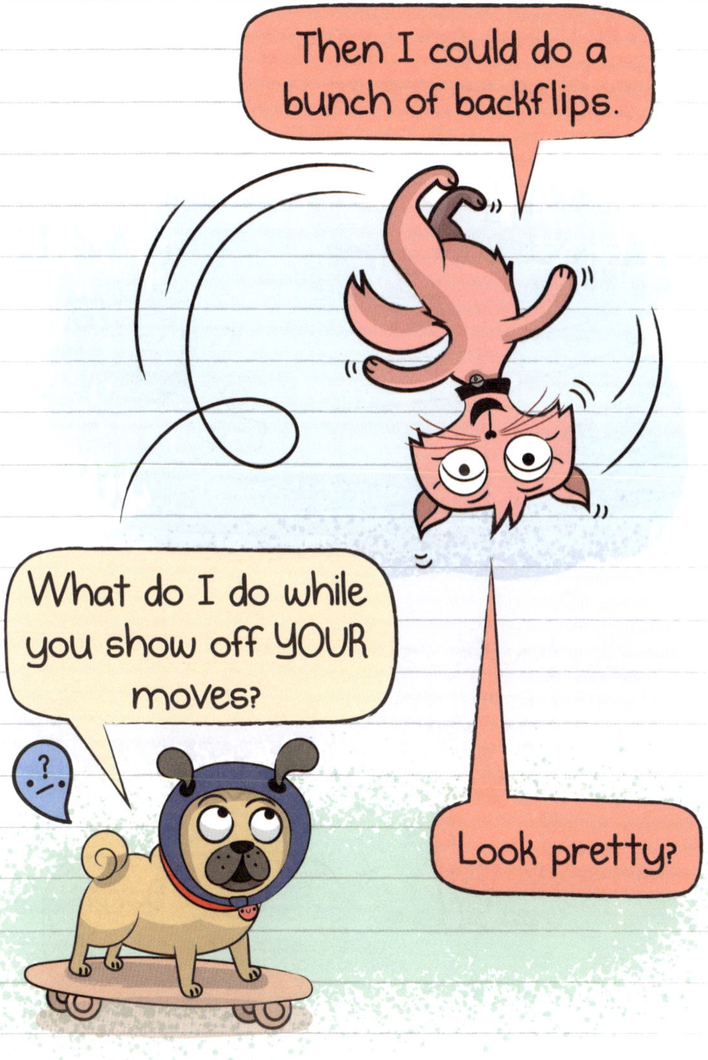

I wondered if I had made a mistake inviting Duchess to be in my act. What if everyone watches her instead of me, Diary? But the act IS more exciting now, and Duchess seems so happy.

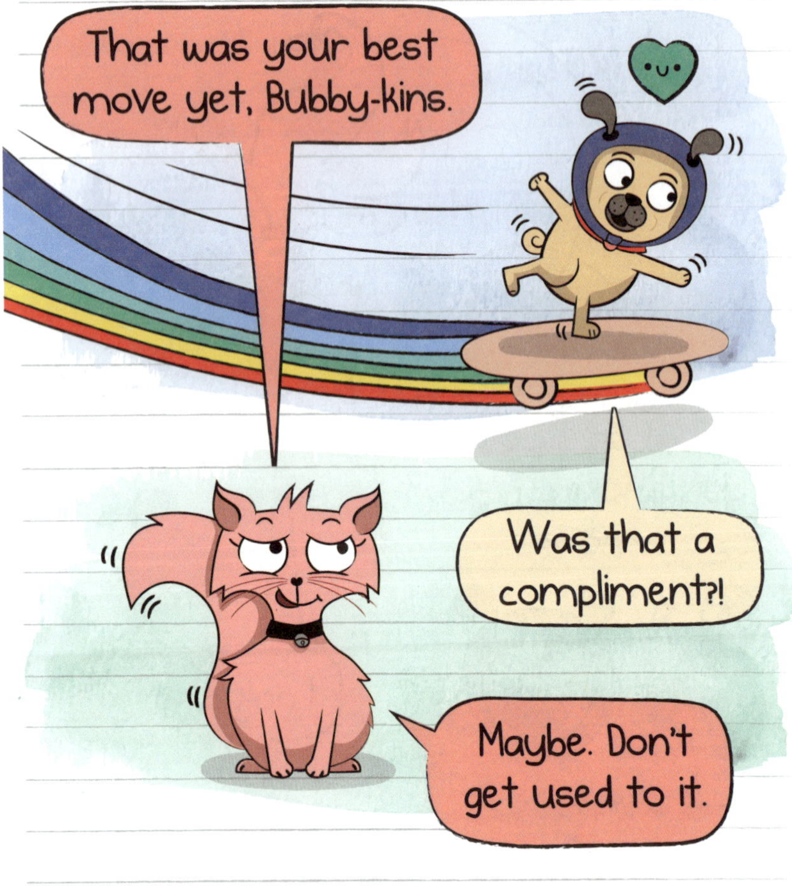

We finished practicing just as Bella came home. Duchess kept walking in circles. She does that when she's nervous.

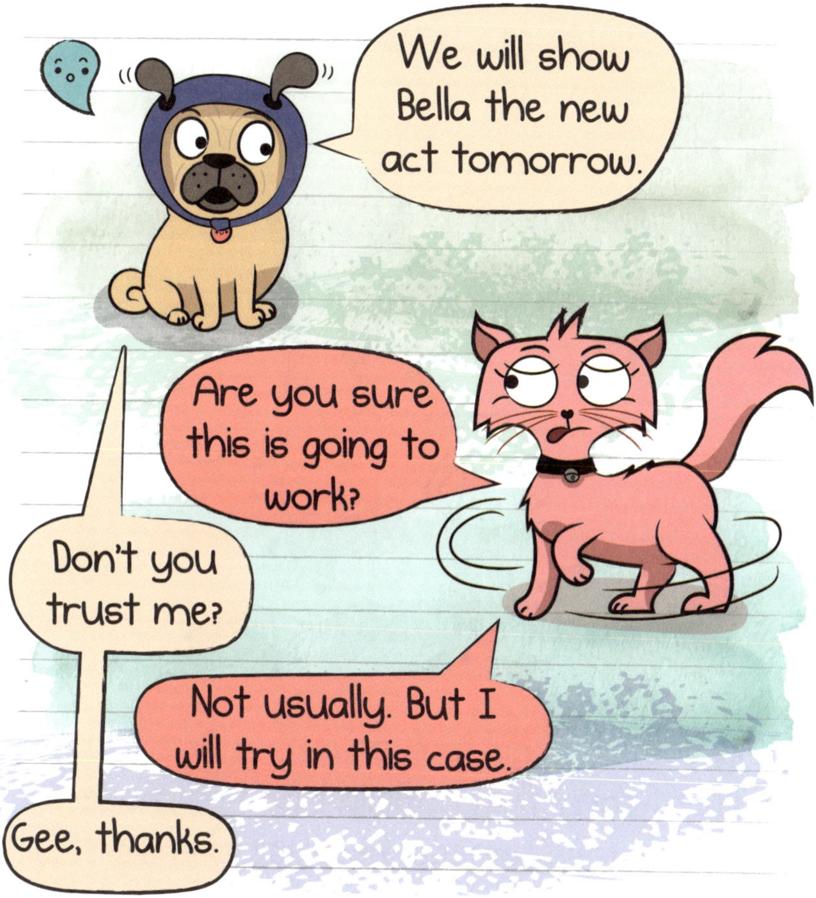

I needed a break from Duchess then, so I went to see what Bella was up to.

She was sewing my costume!

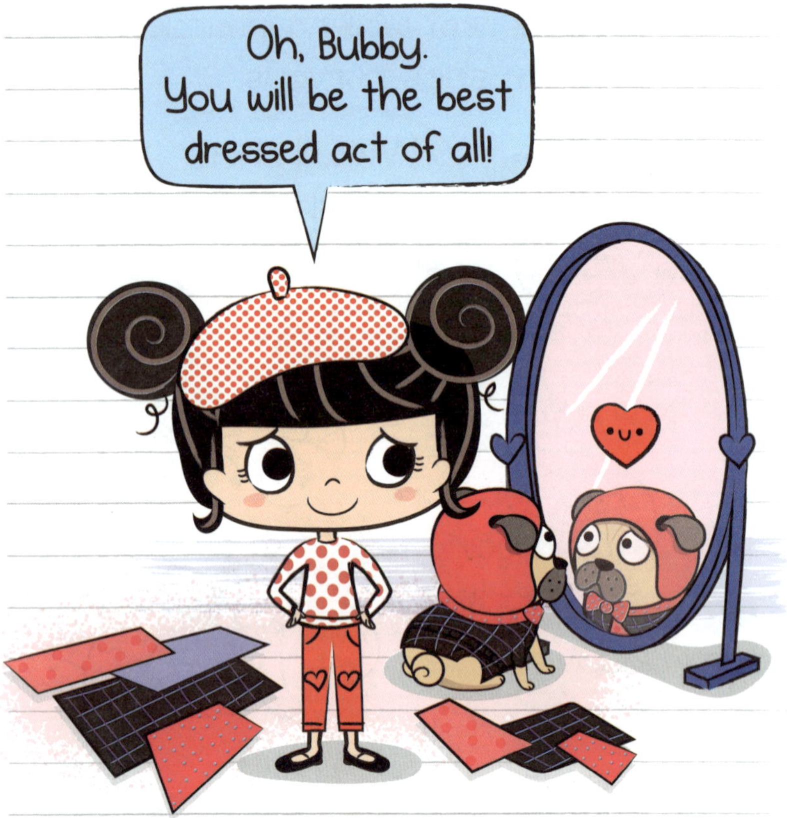

My costume <u>did</u> look stunning. But I realized something... Bella had not made a costume for Duchess, because she didn't know Duchess would be performing! Our act would look silly if only one of us had a costume!

I had to fix this. I waited for Bella to fall asleep. Then I snuck over to the scrap pile. Maybe I could make Duchess an outfit.

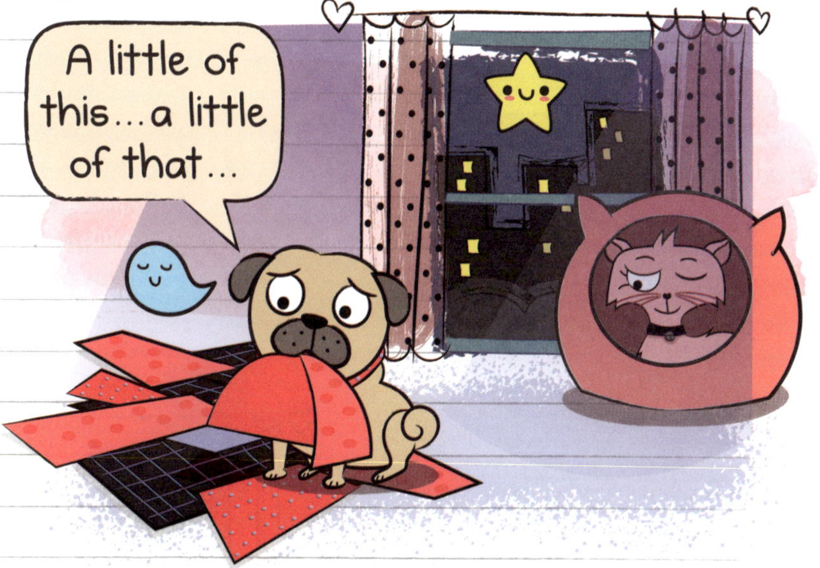

But I was tired and the scrap pile was so comfy.

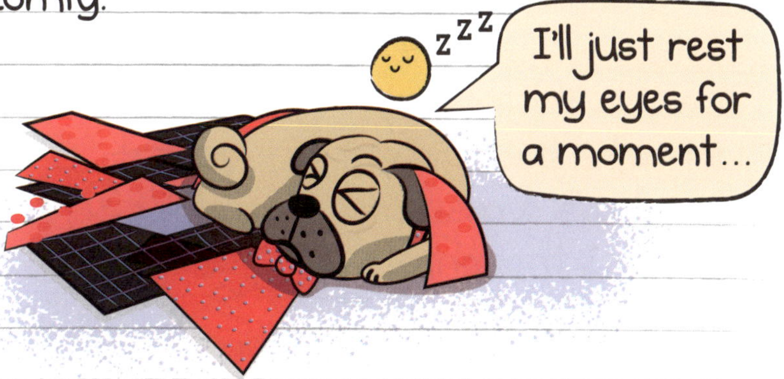

Chapter 7

THE SHOW MUST GO ON

FRIDAY

Dear Diary,

Today was dress rehearsal. ("Dress rehearsal" is showbiz for "practice run with costumes".) But I fell asleep in the scrap pile last night! Duchess still didn't have a costume!

Or so I thought…

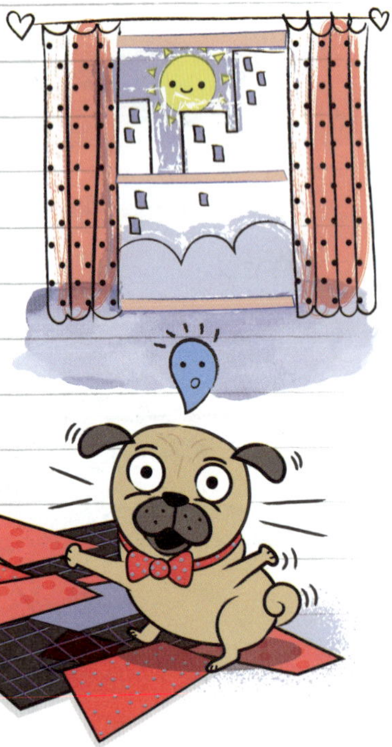

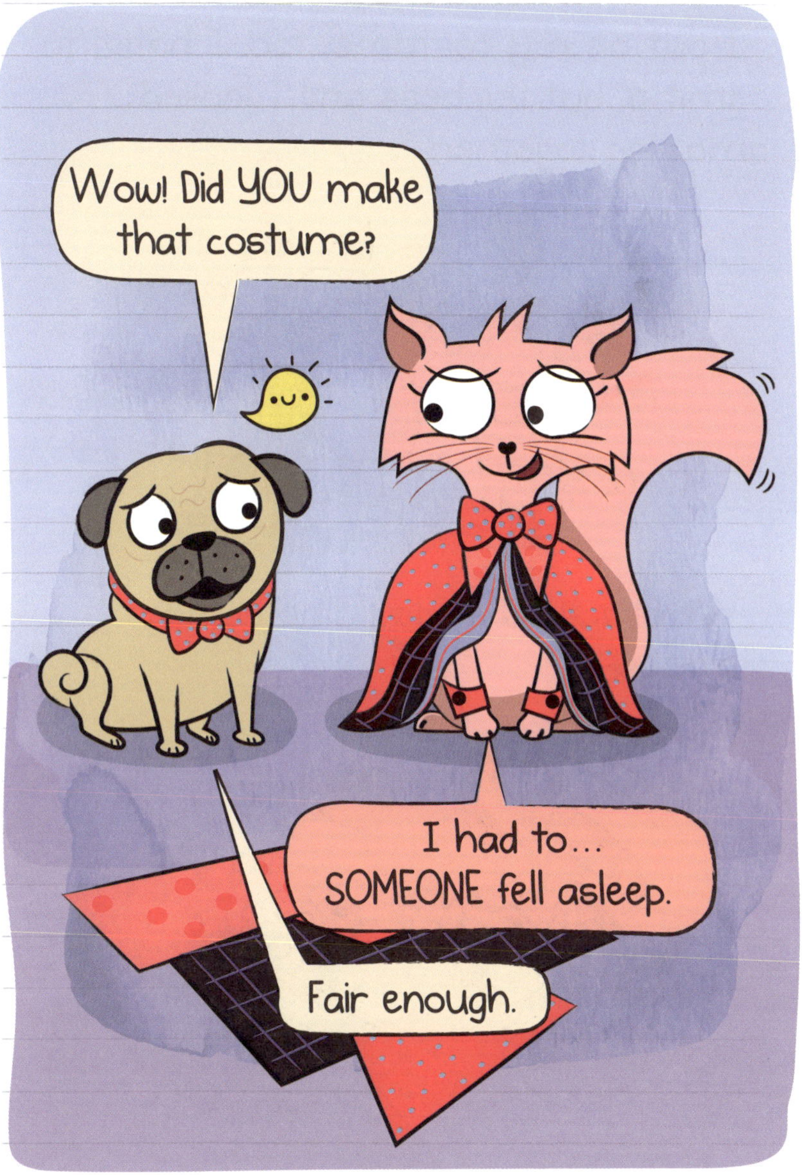
Wow! Did YOU make that costume?
I had to... SOMEONE fell asleep.
Fair enough.

I put on my costume, too. I hated to admit it, but Duchess and I looked amazing together.

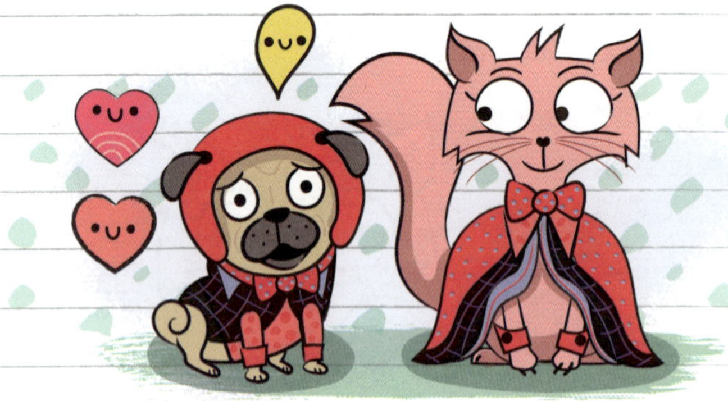

We practiced all day. The act was flawless!

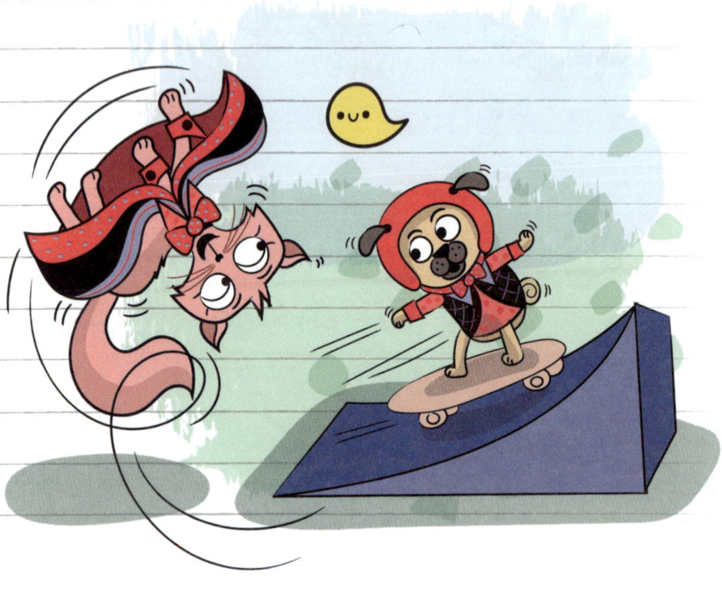

When Bella and Jack got home, it was time for dress rehearsal to start. All the performers gathered backstage. For some reason, Nutz was there, too.

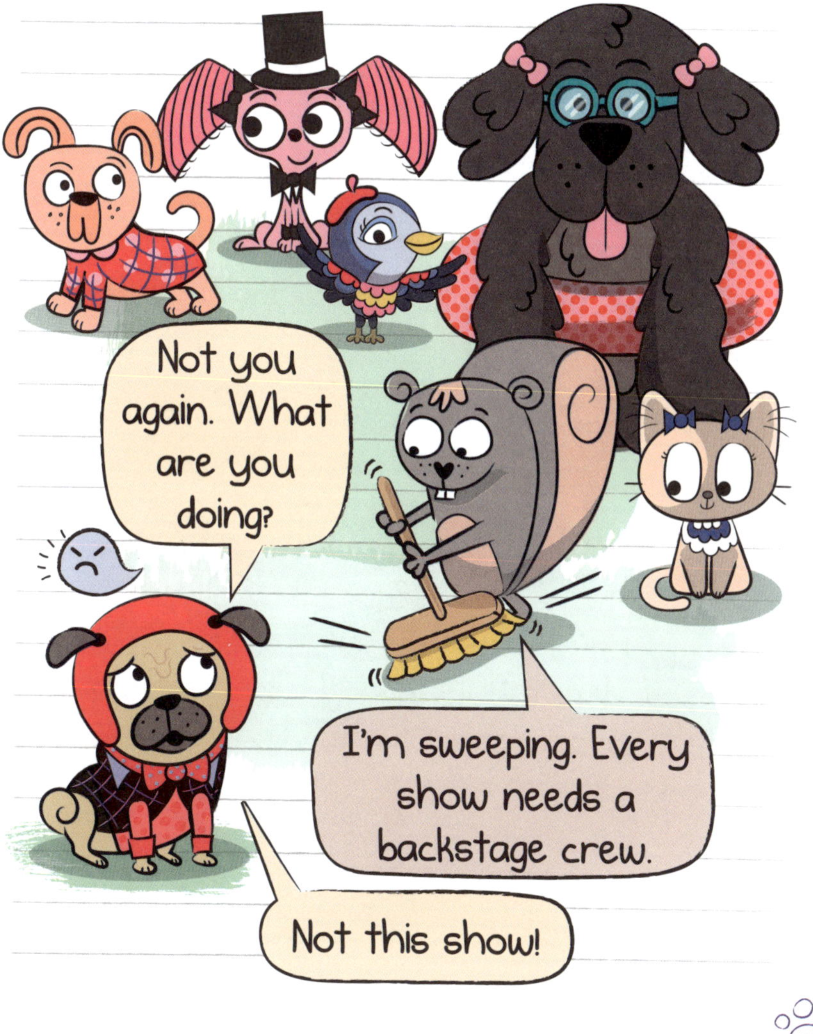

Duchess and I waited backstage for Bella to introduce my act. This was it—how would Bella react to Duchess's surprise appearance? I rolled onstage when Bella called my name.

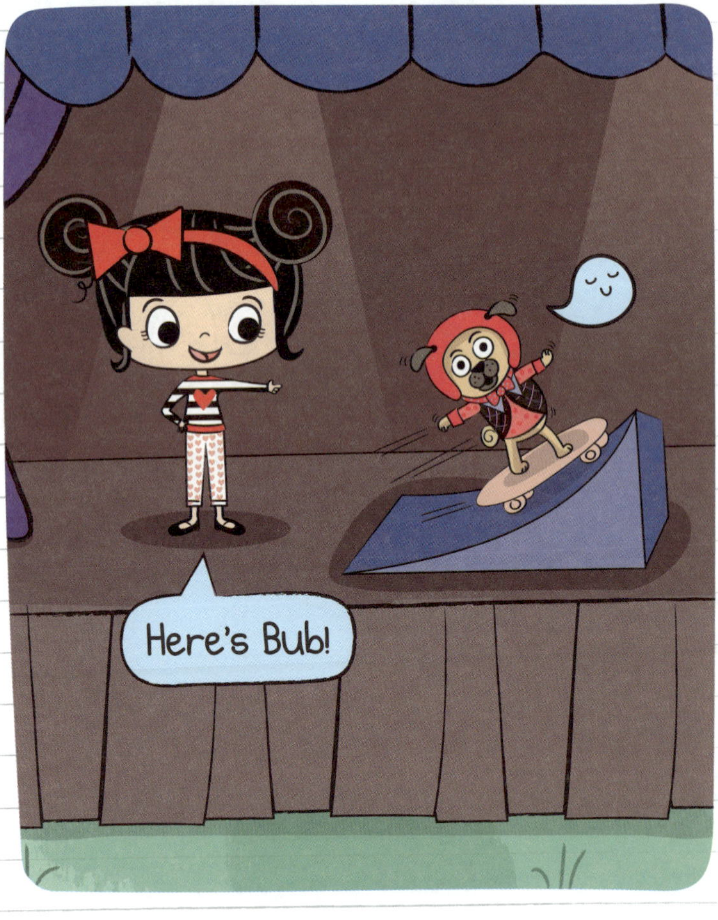

I did a stunt, rolled offstage, and picked up Duchess. Then we both rolled back onstage.

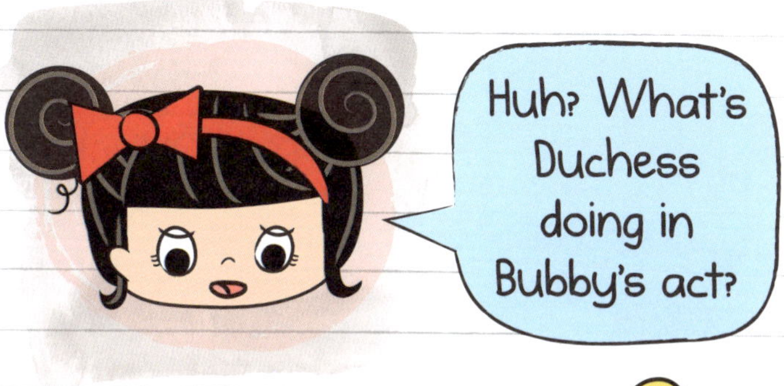

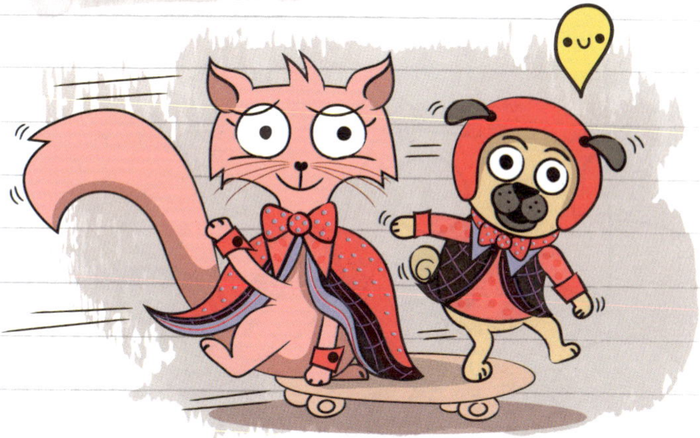

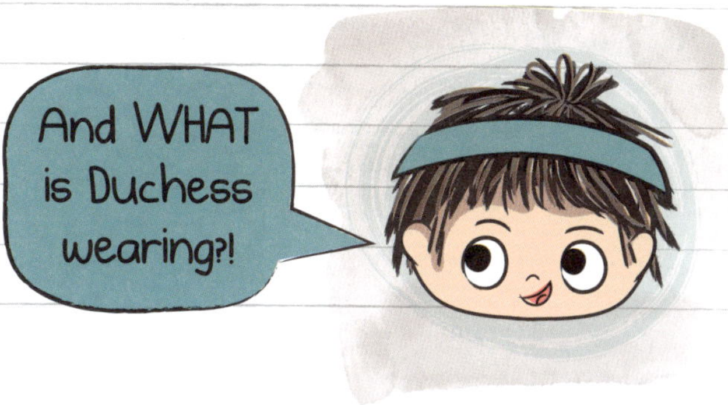

I waited for Duchess to do her triple flip. But she didn't move. She was FROZEN in place!

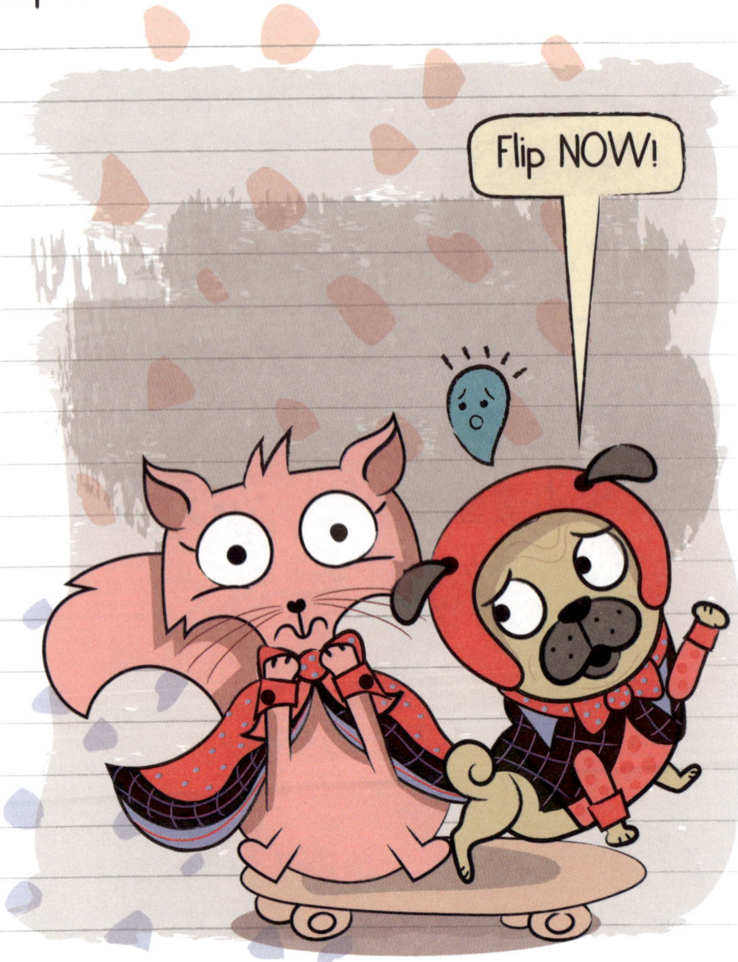

Just then, the puppies ran across the stage. Nutz was chasing them!

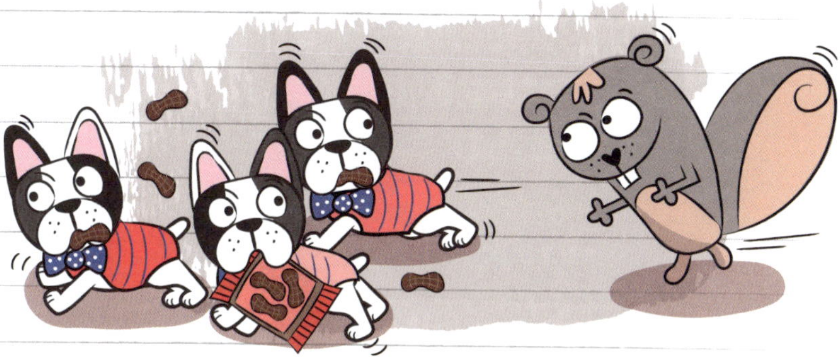

The chase made Duchess snap out of her daze. She freaked out and ran offstage.

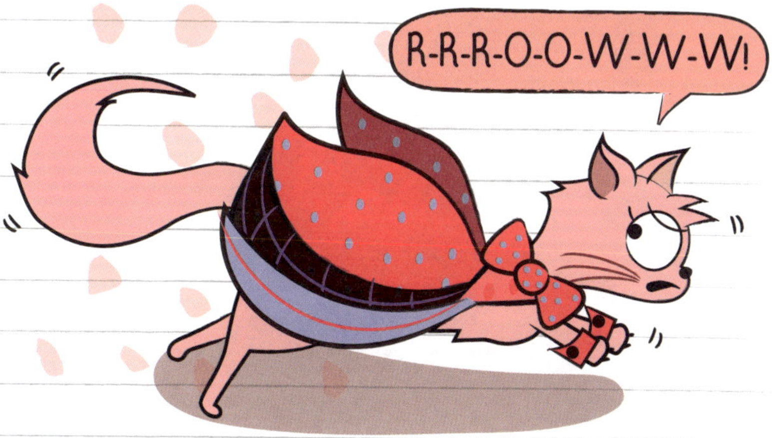

Duchess was so freaked out, she ran into Luna's ladder. It fell over and hit the pool.

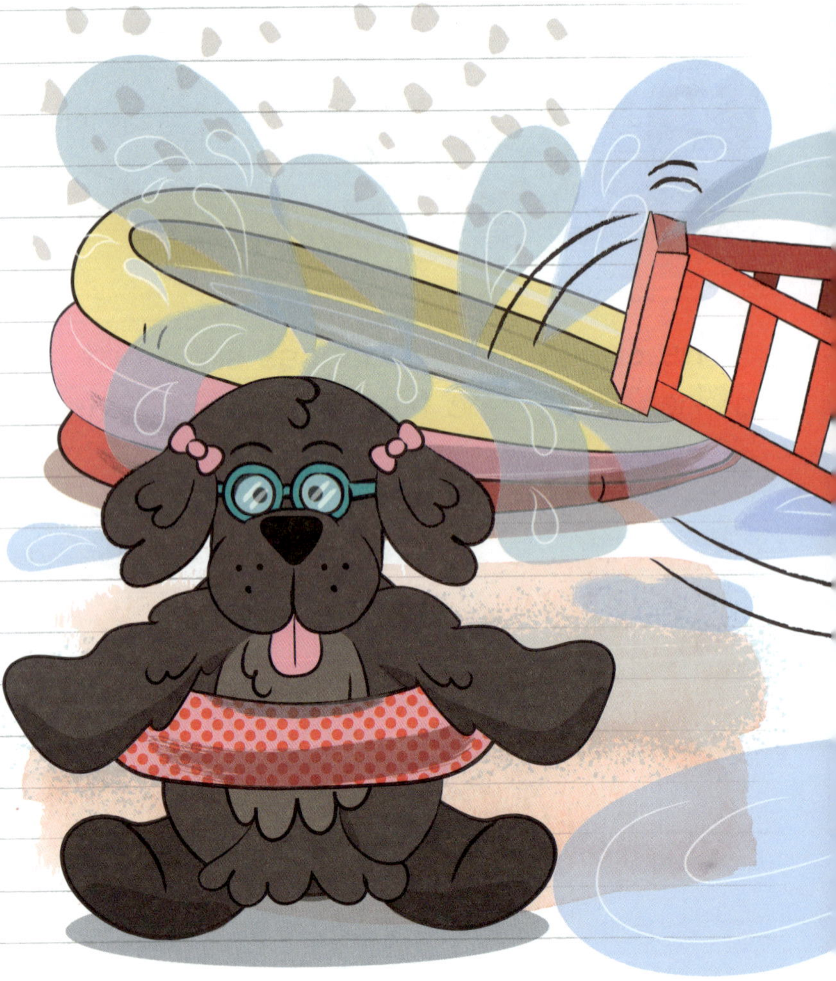

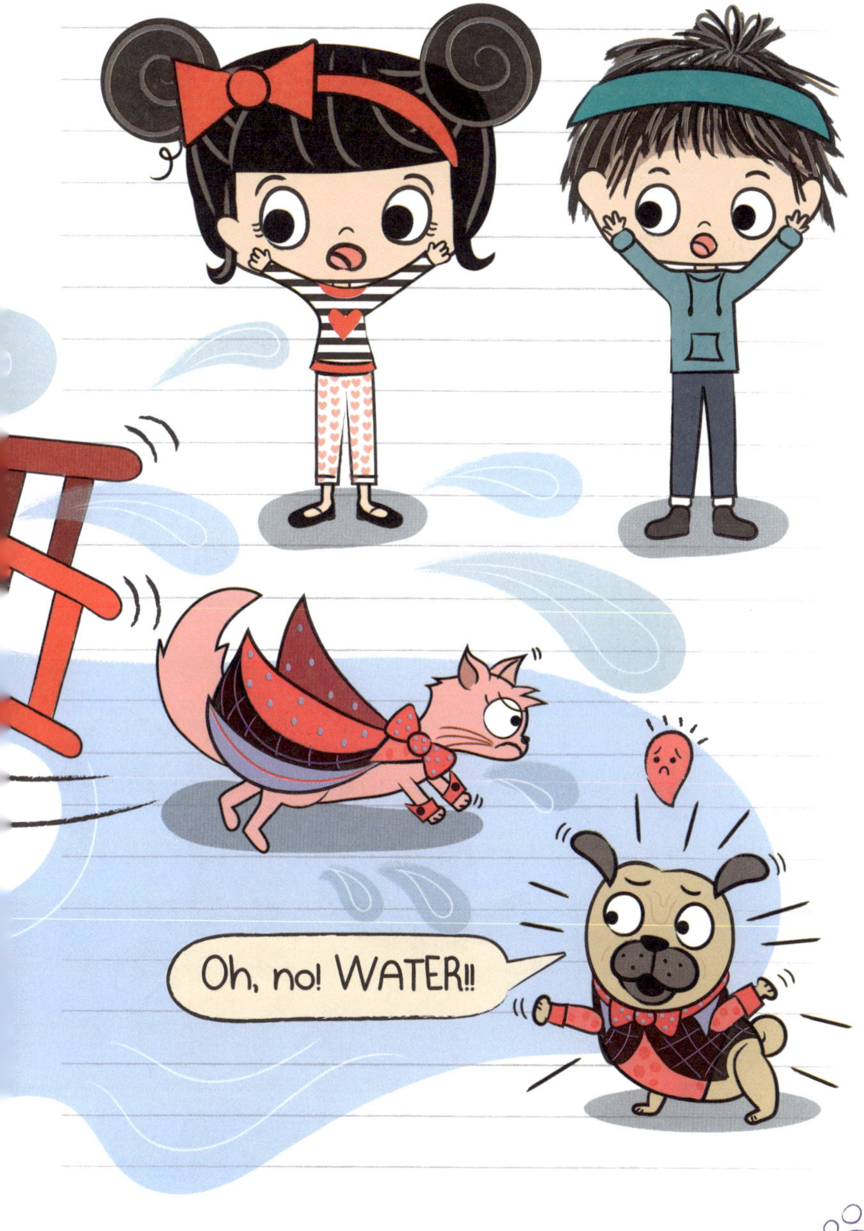
Oh, no! WATER!!

The stage was flooded. There was no way we could practice the rest of the show. Bella sent everyone home.

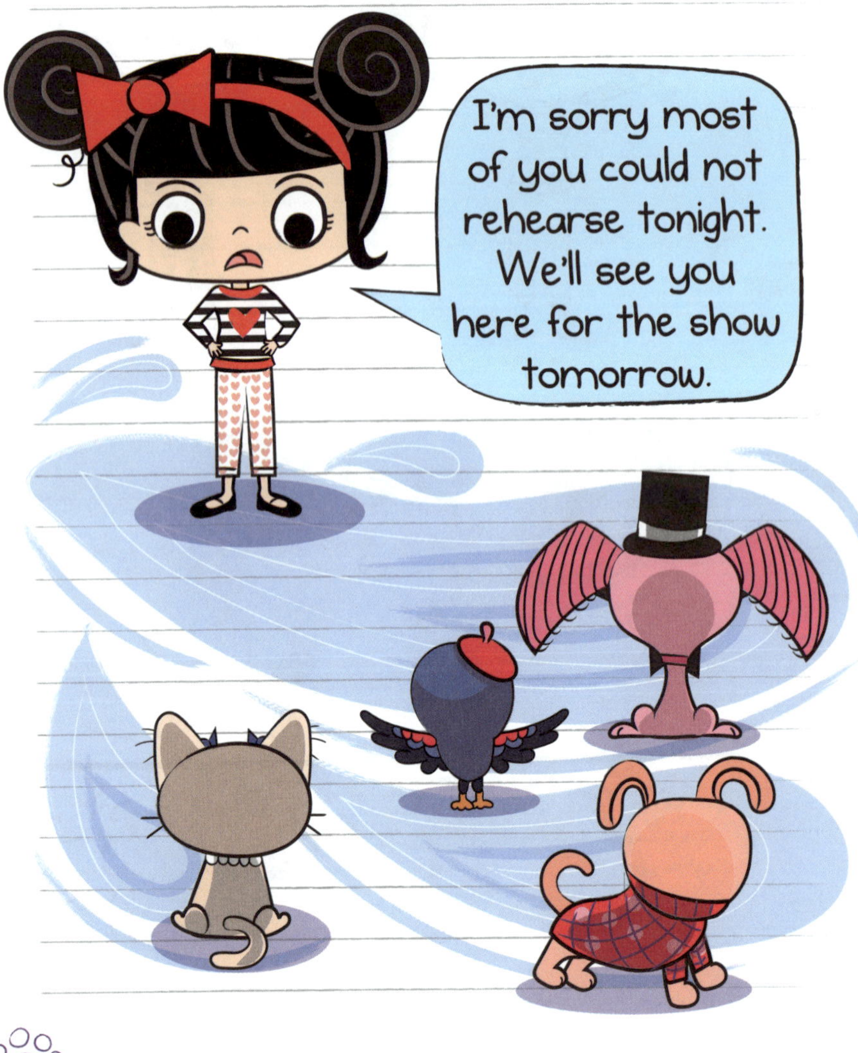

Bella was worried as we cleaned the stage. I felt awful.

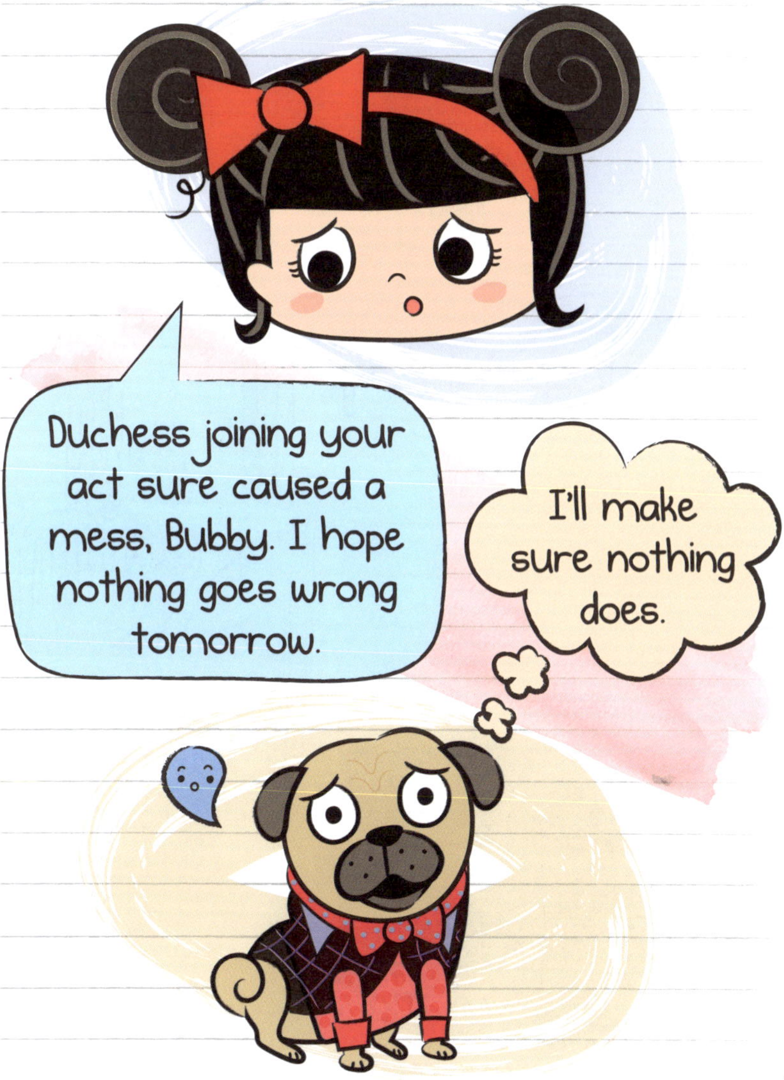

Later, I searched for Duchess. I wanted to understand what happened to her onstage. But I couldn't find her.

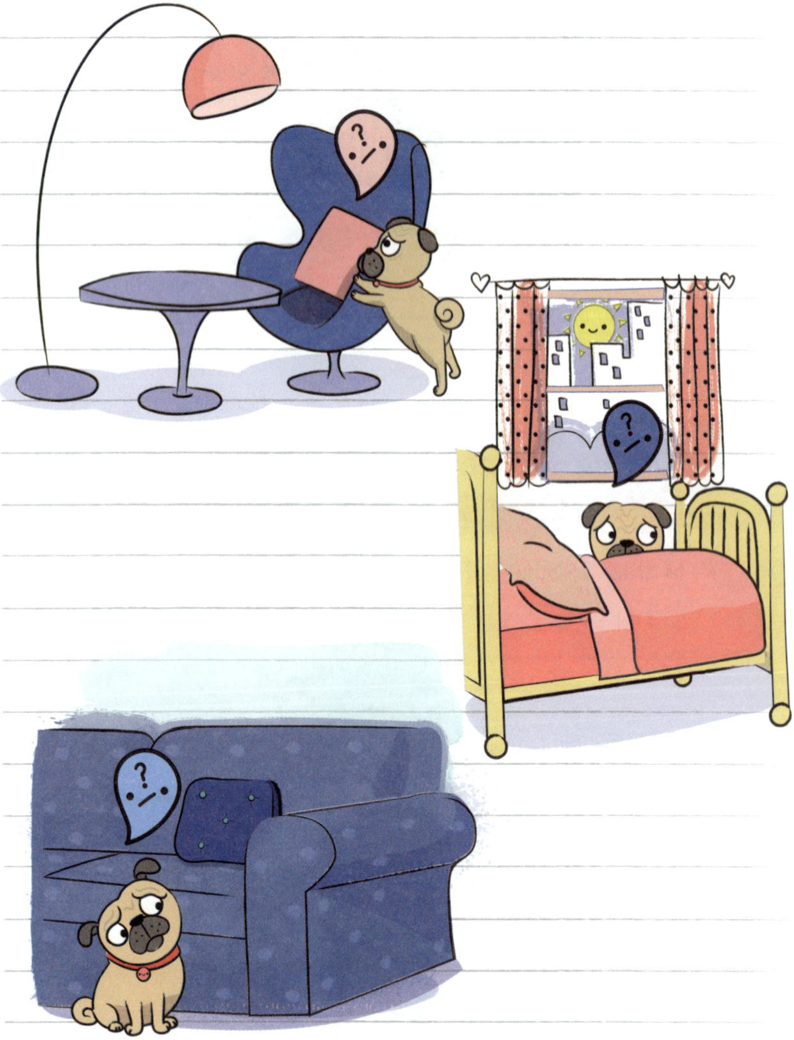

I did find Nutz, though.

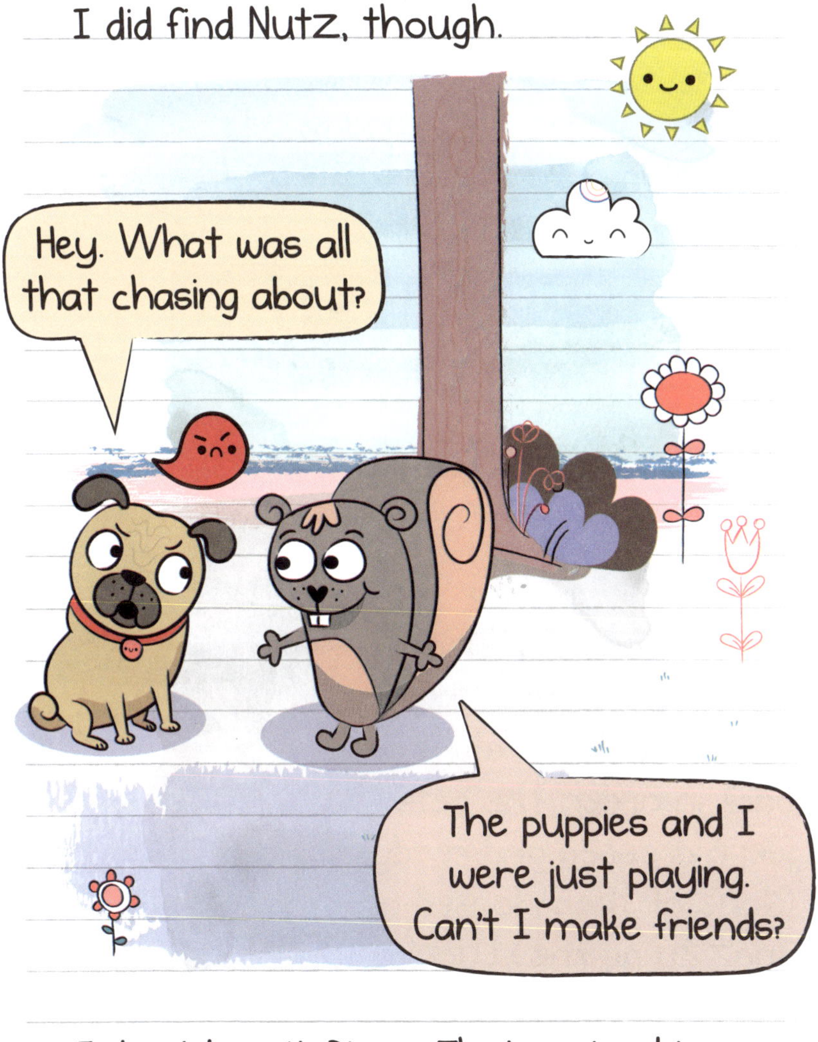

I don't buy it, Diary. That squirrel is up to something. I guess we'll find out at the show tomorrow . . .

Chapter 8

SHOWTIME

SATURDAY

Dear Diary,

Today was the block party, and it was finally SHOWTIME! The stage was back in order. The pets were dressed and ready. (None of them looked as snazzy as me.) Luckily, Nutz was nowhere to be seen. I still couldn't find Duchess. Would I have to do the act alone?

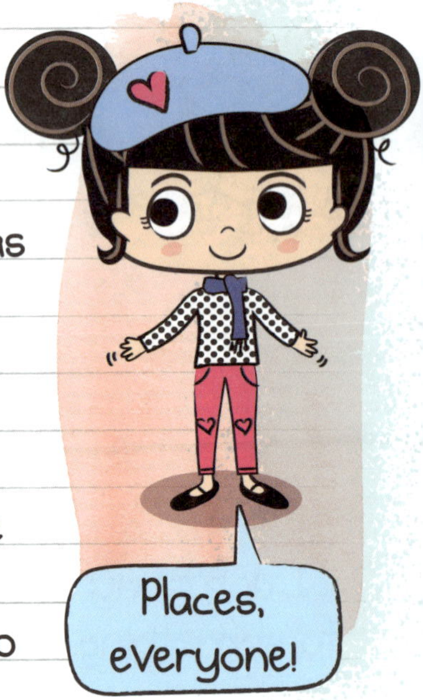

I peeked out from behind the curtain. There were a lot of people in the audience. I got a little nervous. All of a sudden, Duchess appeared.

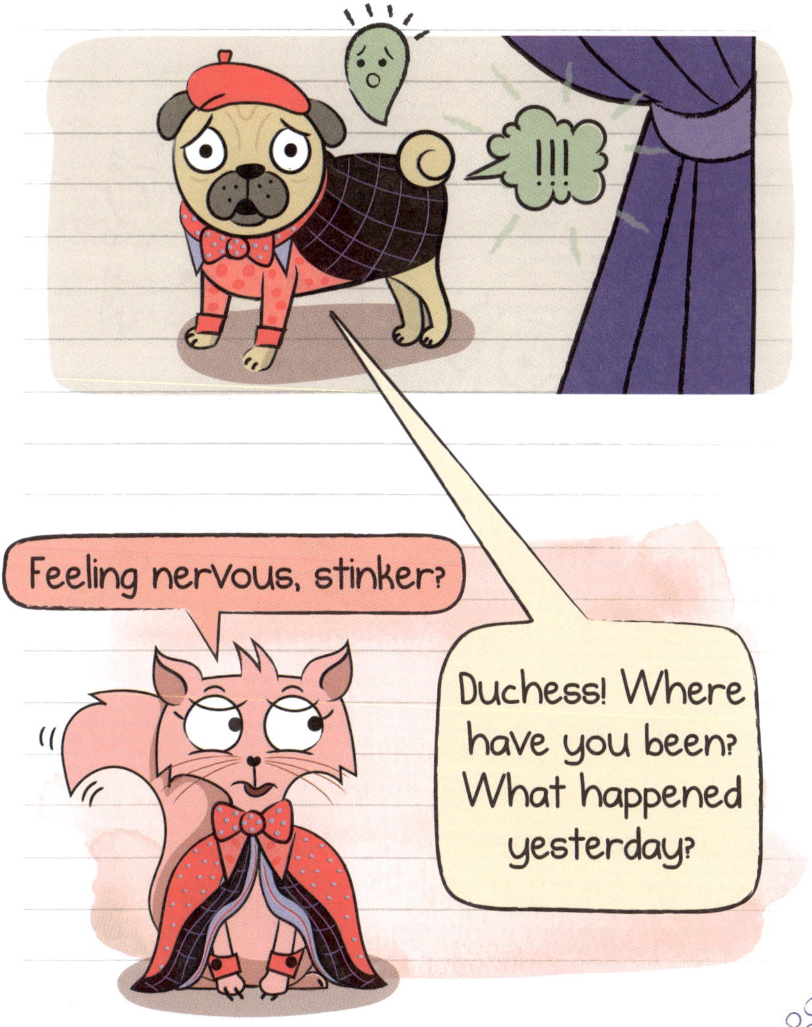

Her answer surprised me. It was an apology!

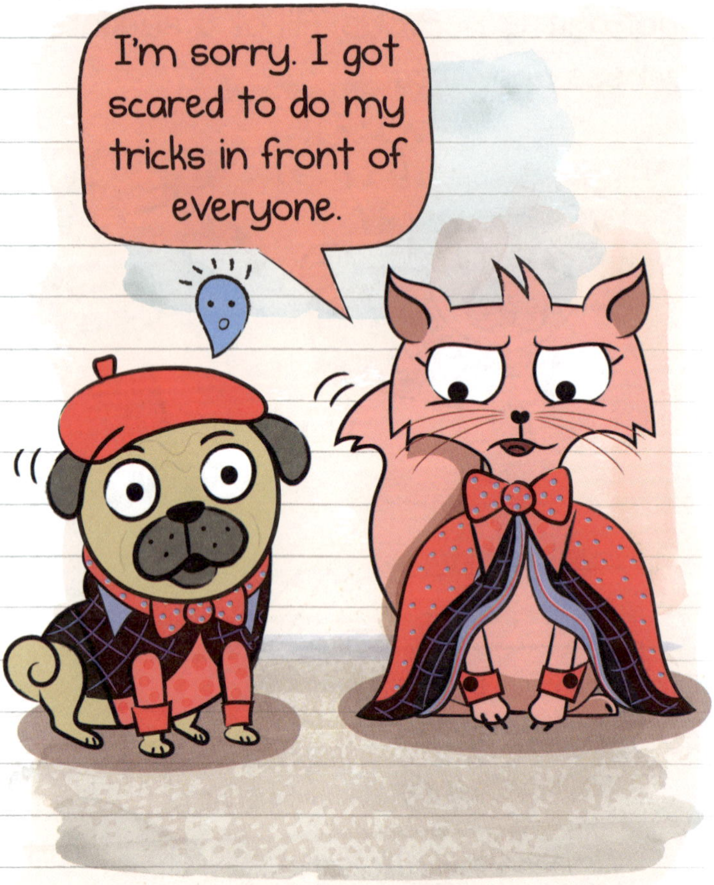

I was speechless, Diary. Duchess had stage fright?! But she is the queen of confidence.

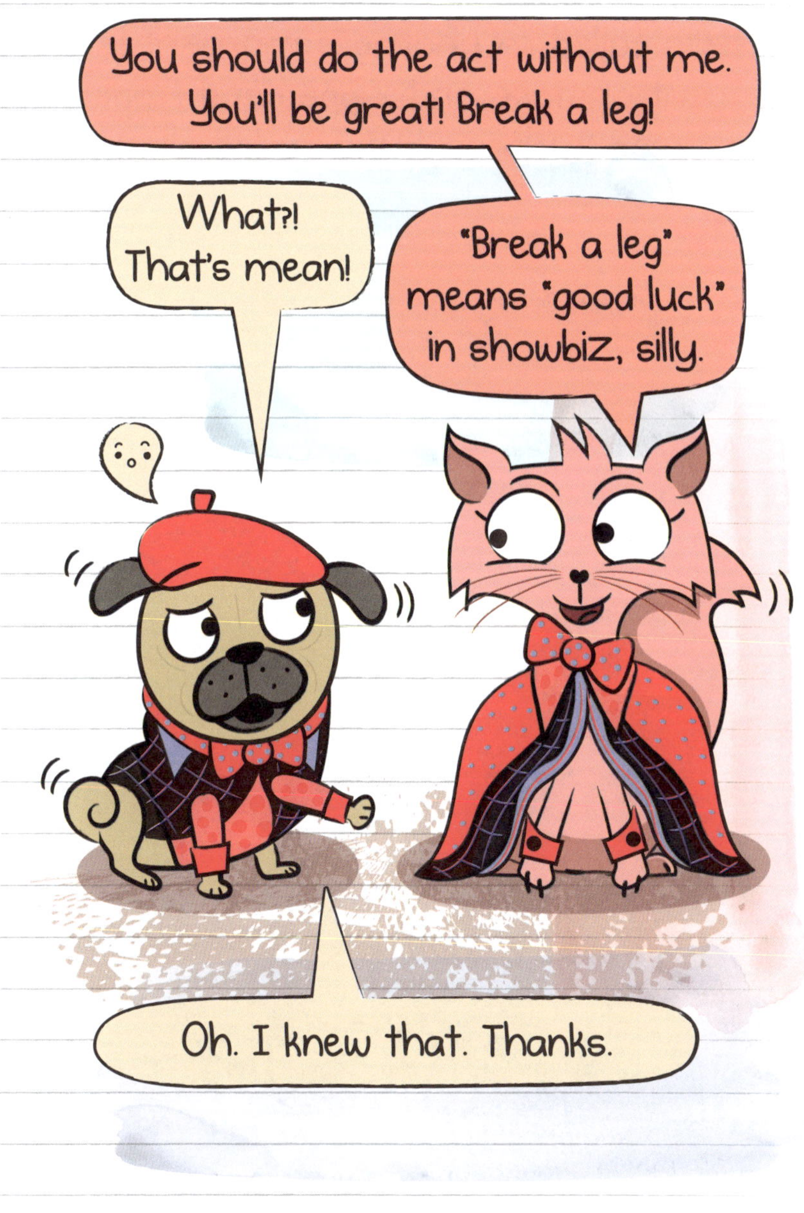
You should do the act without me. You'll be great! Break a leg!
What?! That's mean!
"Break a leg" means "good luck" in showbiz, silly.
Oh. I knew that. Thanks.

Bella called my name a moment later. I went onstage and zipped and flipped. I missed Duchess, but I nailed all my tricks.

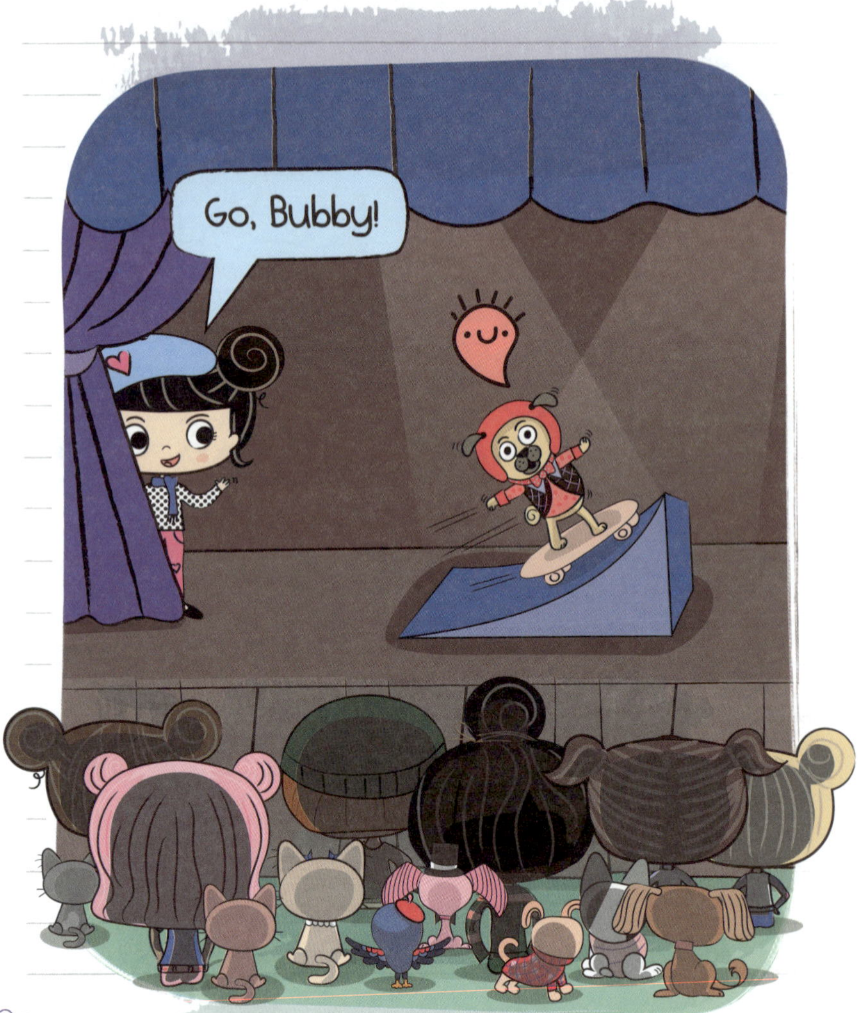

The rest of the show was fabulous. I even stayed dry during Luna's high-dive! We were down to our final act—the puppies and their treats.

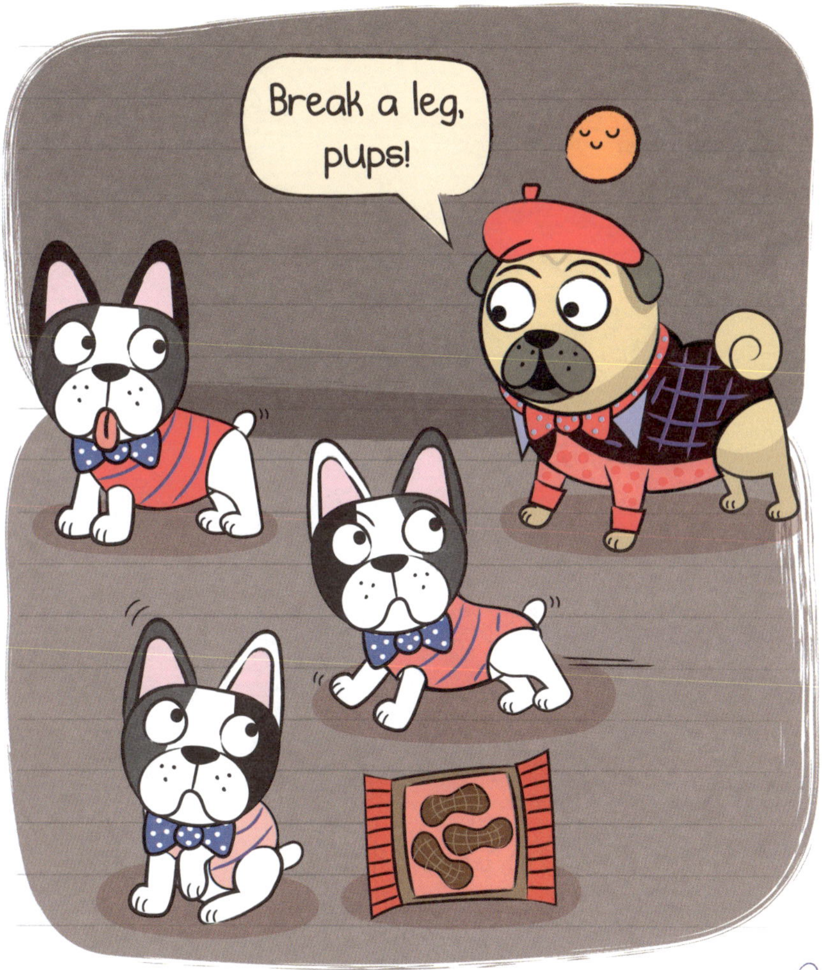

The puppies' act was awesome. But halfway through, Duchess pointed to something. Nutz!

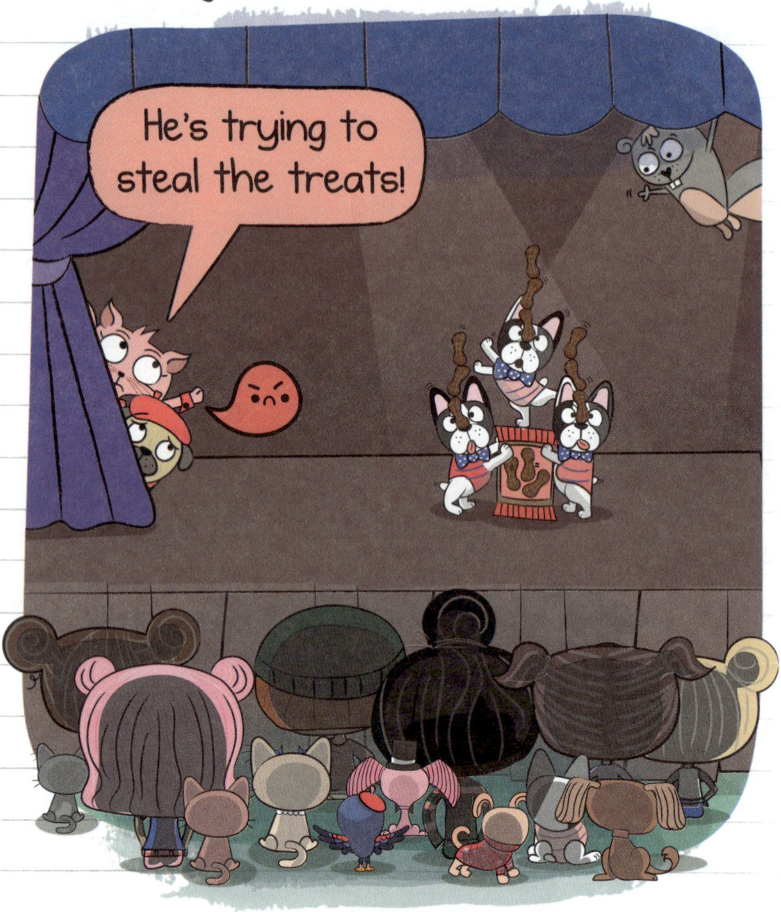

Of course he was, Diary. We had to stop him before he ruined the show!

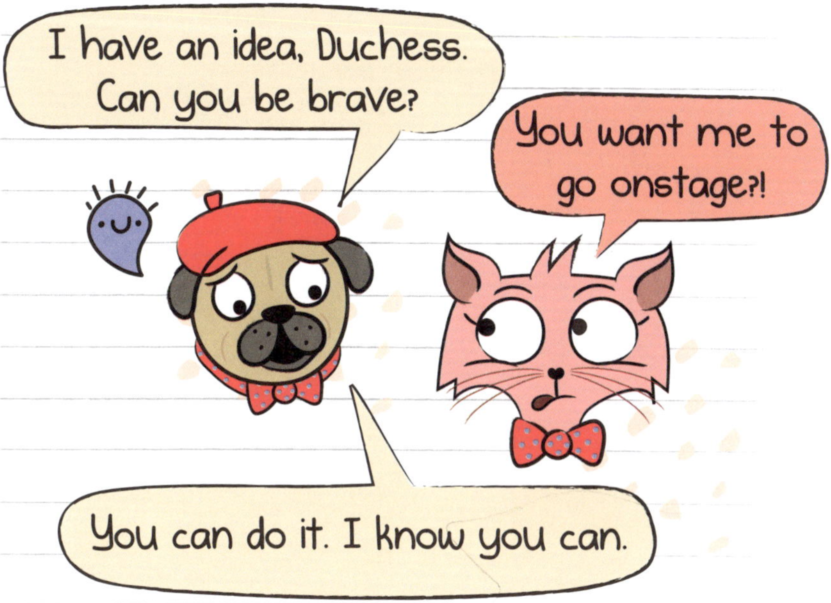

I told her my plan. Then I grabbed my skateboard.

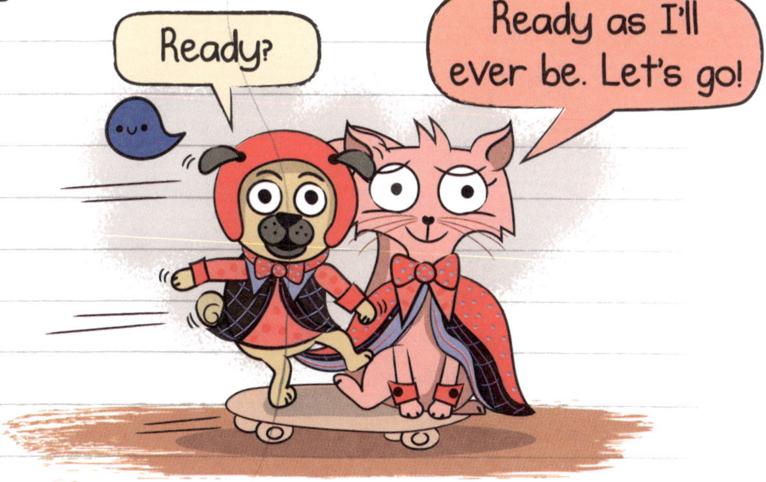

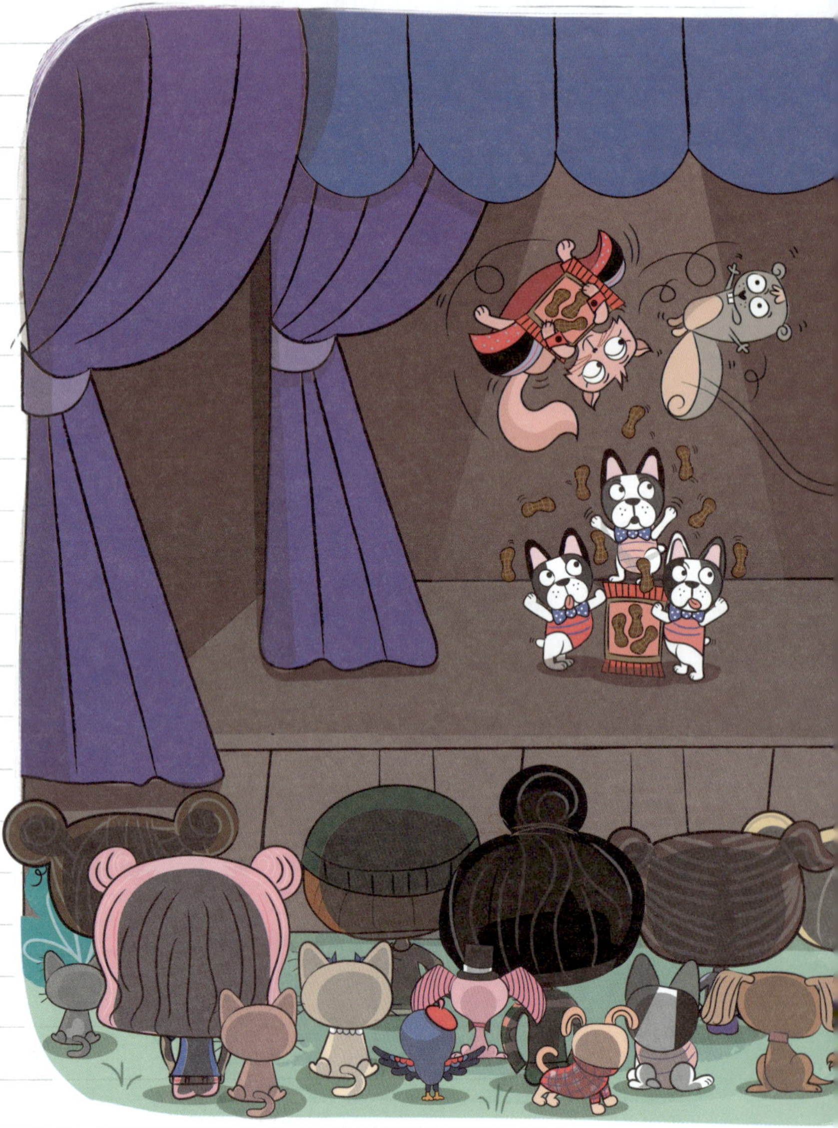

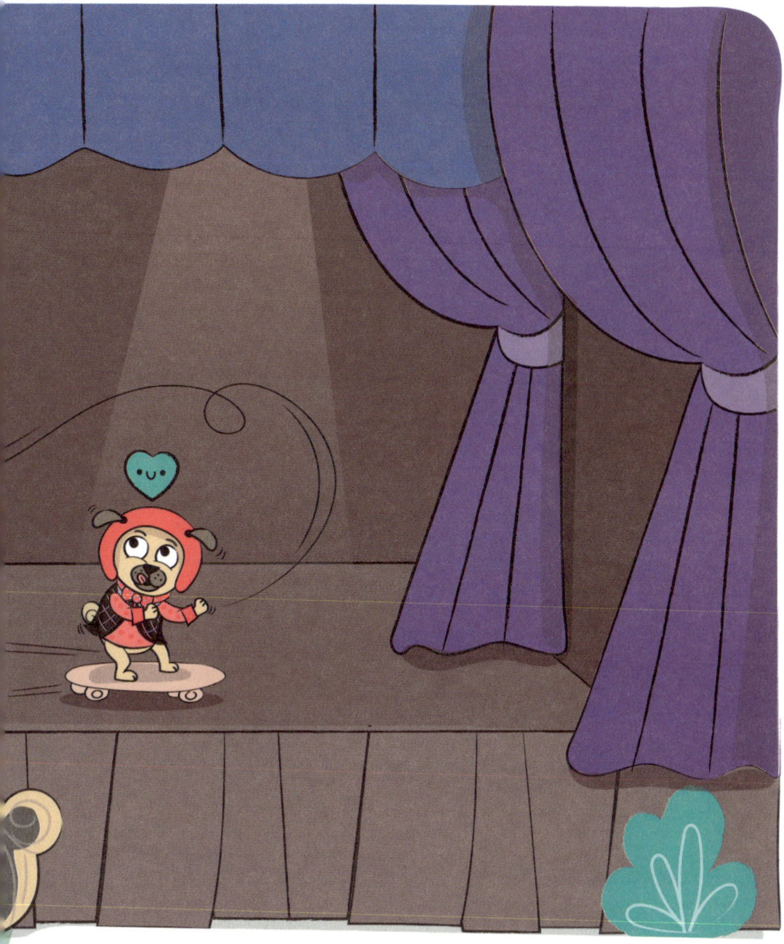

Duchess landed as the puppies finished. It was like we were always part of their act! We saved the treats AND the show. The crowd went wild.

After the show, we all celebrated together.

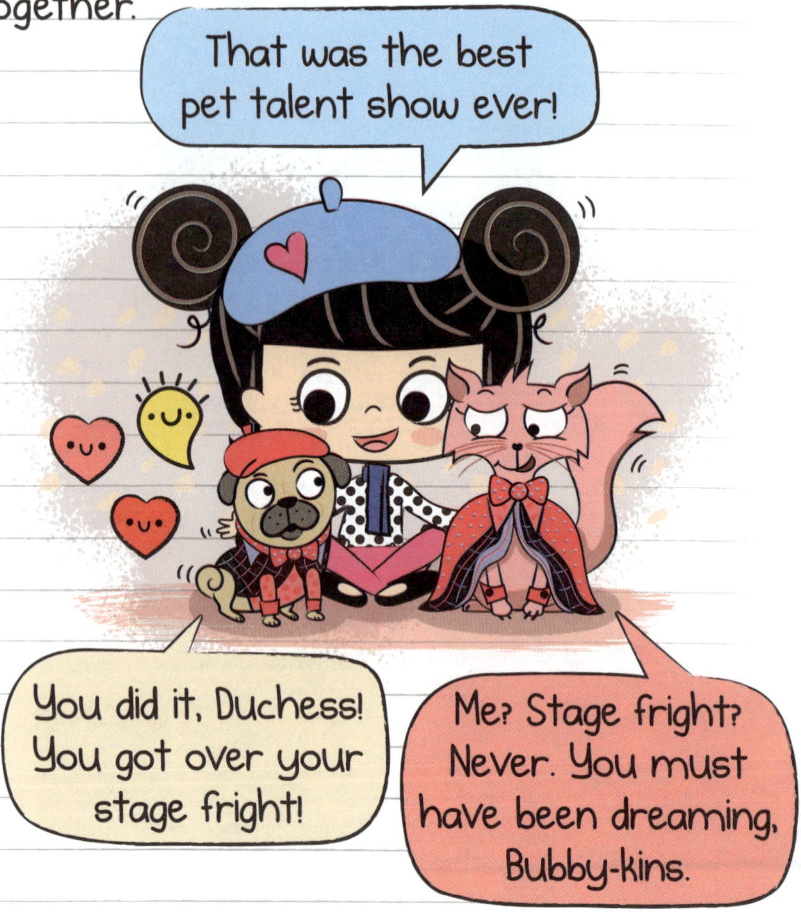

Oh Diary, that cat gets on my nerves! But you know what? We are already planning our act for next year. We might even ask Nutz to join us!

HOW MUCH DO YOU KNOW ABOUT

DIARY OF A PUG

Pug's Got Talent?

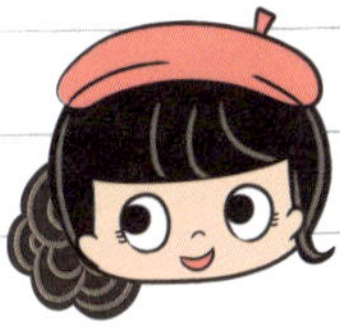

What gives me the idea for a pet talent show?

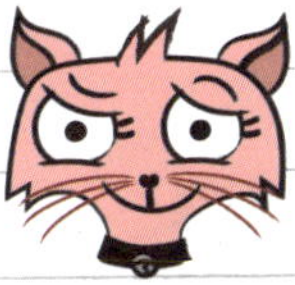

When Bella first shares her idea for a pet talent show, Bub is excited to do his stunts. Why else is Bub excited about the show?

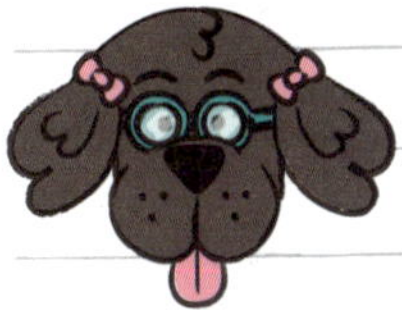

Why does Bub run to hide when I go onstage to practice my act?

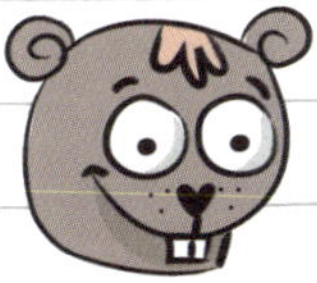

When Duchess is frozen onstage, what snaps her out of her daze?

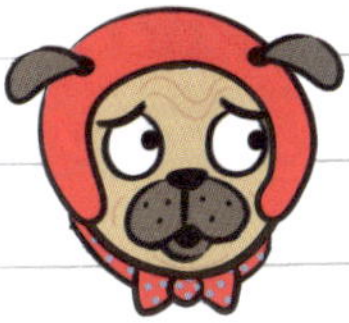

If you were performing in a talent show, what talent would you show off? Draw a picture of yourself performing. Don't forget your costume!

scholastic.com/branches

About the Creator

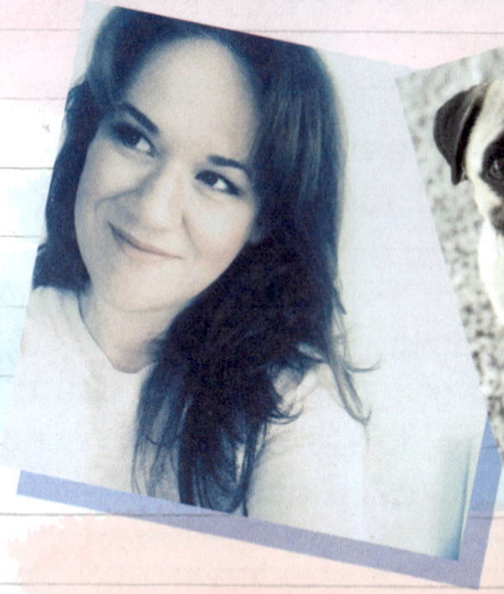

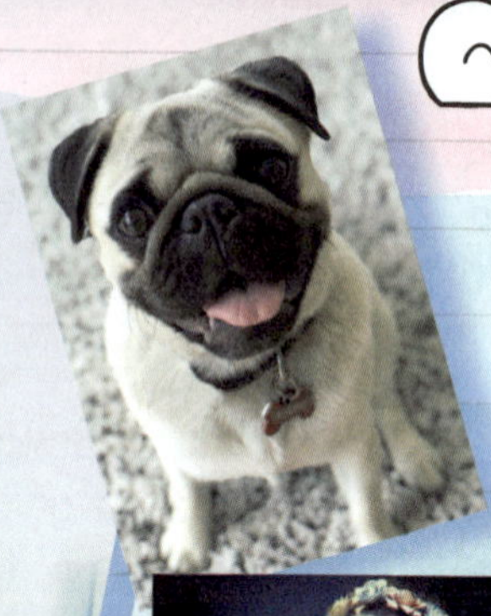

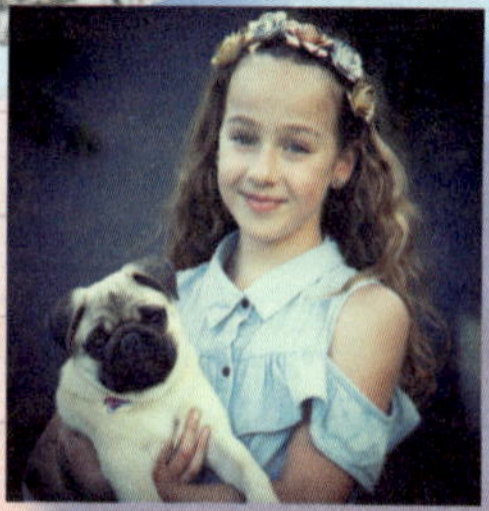

kylamay

Kyla May is an Australian illustrator, writer, and designer. In addition to books, Kyla creates animation. She lives by the beach in Victoria, Australia, with her three daughters and two pups. The character of Bub was inspired by her daughter's pug called Bear.